Editorial

This is an age of manifest – and manifested – sensitivities. We are alerted to cultural, sexual and medical improprieties of expression. We need to protect readers, as listeners and viewers are generally protected, against what may shock or unsettle them. Radio listeners are warned of the proximity of 'strong language' (which indicates obscenity or aggression, a rather gendered notion of 'strong'); television viewers are cautioned against flashing lights which might set off a life-threatening reflex, but also alerted to nudity and sometimes to sexual content. If they choose to over-ride trigger warnings and something they see or hear unsettles them, they're provided with numbers to call or websites to visit. They can be repaired after damage or comforted after hurt. Soap operas are especially considerate in this way.

Magazines, newspapers, books and social media are now commonly in the firing line, though they often hold the gun to their own heads and hearts. To read modern apologies from those who offend, or fear they may have offended, is like reading accounts of abasement in imperial Rome. If you fell foul of the Emperor, you demeaned yourself, and when you could go no lower you finished yourself off, leaving your estate to your master. Nero's great tutor Seneca is a startling example, having taken obedience and obeisance to the nth degree. The emperor was generally unaccountable, until the Praetorian Guard turned. When a modern writer is caught out, there are often in print accounts to settle.

The different types of rhetoric surrounding the case of *Some Kids I Taught and What They Taught Me* (2019) by the poet, anthologist and teacher Kate Clanchy are familiar. She deployed – unmaliciously, but carelessly – epithets in her book which propagated racial and other stereotypes. An attentive editor might have queried them, but no such person was on hand. Few critics noticed them when the book appeared, was widely praised, and received the Orwell Prize for political writing, becoming a best-seller. When, earlier this year, readers began to question the poet's specific language on Goodreads, they were themselves – Chimene Suleyman, Monisha Rajesh and Professor Sunny Singh in particular – stereotyped and denounced in the social media.

This helped characterise the poet's support culture as itself racist, especially when, after first denying that she had used the epithets she was taxed with, she had to climb down – because they were there in her book in black and white. There followed a rush for the exit: individuals and journals that had given her support or editorial houseroom turned on her and then began to *mea culpa* themselves. The poet, too, undertook an act of public contrition. It will culminate in her rewriting the offending passages and maybe undertaking a more comprehensive rewrite of her book. She may add a new chapter reflecting on her learning curve, inviting us to share her awakening.

A few months ago *Poetry Wales* conducted an interview with the poet, addressing her as 'neurodivergent'. On 9 August they posted an apology 'in regards to [sic] the publication of a conversation with Kate Clanchy in the Summer 2021 edition of the magazine'. 'We are appalled to have since learned that, in her book Some Kids I Taught and What They Taught Me (Picador, 2019), Clanchy uses language and descriptions that we and many others know to be racist and ableist.' They had not read the book in advance of the interview, it would seem, like many of her admirers and critics. In the interview, she did not express racist or ableist views, so it might have been inferred that *Poetry Wales'* readers had been spared. Instead of undertaking In future to do their homework – due preparation, due diligence – and read the books of their interviewees, they proposed a more elaborate approach. 'In line with our work to make our magazine a welcoming and inclusive space, we are establishing new policies to help guide everyone involved in the production, oversight, and management of Poetry Wales to ensure that the content of the magazine truly reflects our aims. A statement and article about this will appear in the forthcoming issue of the magazine. We will continue to work hard to make poetry and poetry resources more accessible, welcoming, and inclusive.' Abjection follows: 'We apologise to our contributors and readers, to everyone who has trusted us, and to all who have been harmed and hurt by *Some Kids I Taught and What They Taught Me*. In publishing the conversation with Clanchy, we contributed to the distress of peers, strangers, and friends. We have undermined our own values by publishing this item, making our magazine a less safe space, especially for writers of colour, disabled writers, and neurodivergent writers, which is entirely the reverse of our aims. Poetry Wales condemns all forms of discrimination including racism, ableism, sexism, homophobia, biphobia, transphobia, Islamophobia, and Antisemitism.'

Clanchy – after claiming she had been misquoted – realised she was on a hiding to nothing. She, too, *mea culpa*ed: 'I am not a good person. I do try to say that in my book. Not a pure person, not a patient person, no one's saviour. You are right to blame me, and I blame myself.' Philip Pullman initially defended the poet and said her detractors might 'find a comfortable home in Isis or the Taliban'. When he realised his mistake, he exclaimed, 'Completely my fault. I should have read the whole thread. I apologise for my haste and intemperate language.'

Picador, the book's publisher, also apologised, twice – first mildly, then vehemently. It said it was listening to the conversations the book had given rise to and was 'profoundly sorry' for the hurt caused to those who had 'engaged with the text' (i.e., read) 'to hold us to account'. 'We realise our response was too slow. We vigorously condemn the despicable online bullying of many of those who have spoken out. This has no place in our community. We understand that readers wish to know specifically what will be done about the book, we're actively working on this now and we will communicate this as soon as possible.' The accumulation of adverbs is an index of contrition.

Set this domestic calling to account, which exposed some unreflective aspects of our contemporary publishing culture, alongside recent developments in other countries. Substantial institutions, religious and political, and the state itself, are putting pressure on publishers and writers – not locally corrective but more fundamentally intended. During lockdown, people had time to read, and those in power had time to oversee and correct their reading. In October last year 847 examples of censorship in various countries were identified by the International Publishers' Association in their report

Freedom to Publish: Challenges, Violations and Countries of Concern. These countries included Hungary, Poland, Russia, Belarus, Serbia, China, Iran, but also France, the UK and the USA. Over half the censorship was perpetrated by governments directly or obliquely. Instances of censorship continue unabated. The targets in Eastern Europe in particular are LGBTQ+ writers and books. Russia leads the way in European censorship, having passed the 'anti-LGBTQ propaganda' law in 2012. Belarus is a vivid flash-point, with the local chapter of International PEN having been disbanded for having exposed 621 human rights violations in a report.

There are many ways of censoring books. Central control of paper supply can be used to penalise publishers who take wrong turnings, as in Venezuela – and Russia. Turkish authorities demand that every book sold in a bookshop should have a sticker declaring it 'authentic'. This is not only to defeat piracy: it is an obvious form of regulation.

One effect of censorship, oblique or manifest, is that it leads to protective self-censorship, not only among librarians and publishers but among writers themselves. Writers' groups can become regulatory. The Society of Children's Book Writers and Illustrators (SCBWI) has more than 22,000 members around the world. In July it issued 'a fervent apology to Muslim and Palestinian members over a recent condemnation of antisemitism that did not discuss Islamophobia, and announced the resignation of the diversity officer who had posted the message.' The offending SCBWI statement on antisemitism, published in June, affirmed that Jews 'have the right to life, safety, and freedom from scapegoating and fear'. Noting the rise in antisemitism and antisemitic violence, it said, 'Silence is often mistaken for acceptance and results in the perpetration of more hatred and violence against different types of people.'

We can be grateful to Chimene Suleyman, Monisha Rajesh, Professor Sunny Singh and others for rejecting silence. What *they* taught *us* is valuable going forward.

Letter

On the translation of 'Ouvroir de littérature potentielle' in the article on the Oulipo group
'Workshop of potential literature' is a good, but debatable translation. It does cling to 'first meanings' of the originals, which are perhaps not intended. A French workshop is properly *un atelier*, which is also a studio. An *ouvroir* is a workspace or sewing corner. The *atelier* of a

craftsman would produce finished goods; an *ouvroir* is a transitory, domestic, and less formal environment. The 'first meaning' of the word '*potentiel*' is certainly English 'potential', as in 'possible'. But it's more philosophical denotation is 'aspiring', 'imminent' or 'aspirational'.

Thus, perhaps one other translation would be 'Workspace for imminent writing'. – *W. Bruno*

A Note on the Cover

After two years of restraint, *PN Review* is returning to pictorial covers. This and the next five issues (the whole of Volume 48) will have cover images by poet and artist Gregory O'Brien. His poems have been published in *PNR* and

he has provided vivid cover images down the decades, starting with *PNR* 111, 'Aviator Fallen in a Desert', acrylic and ink on paper (September–October 1996, exactly twenty-five years ago).

News & Notes

Jean 'Binta' Breeze · the Jamaican-American poet died in August at the age of sixty-five. We will publish a celebration of her by SuAndi in *PNR* 262. Her British publisher, Bloodaxe, describe her in these terms: 'Jean's performances were so powerful that she was called "a one-woman festival", a testament also to the way in which she fully embodied the characters she brought to life in her poems, male as well as female.'

Jaan Kaplinski · one of Estonia's outstanding poets and cultural figures died in August at the age of eighty-one. Born in Tartu shortly after the Soviet Union annexed Estonia, to an Estonian mother and a Polish-Jewish father, he described the repression, fear and poverty in which he grew up. His father starved to death in a Soviet labour camp, having been a professor of philology at the University of Tartu. Jaan became a student and then a scholar of Romance languages and linguistics. He lectured on the History of Western Civilisation at Tartu and studied Mahayana Buddhism and philosophies of the Far East. He published collections of poetry and essays in Estonian, Finnish and English, and in more recent years he wrote Russian, also, producing a collection of poems in 2014. His work has been widely translated. Gary Snyder said, 'he is re-thinking Europe, revisioning history, in these poems of our times. Elegant, musing, relentless, inward, fresh. Poems of gentle politics and love that sometimes scare you.' His British publishers include Bloodaxe who in 2004

published *Evening Brings Everything Back* and *Selected Poems* (2011).

Esmail Khoi · the exiled Iranian poet who lived in the United Kingdom and upheld the tradition of the great Persian writers of the middle ages died in London in June at the age of eighty-two. He lived to regret his support for the Islamic Revolution (he had opposed the Shah and came to oppose the theocratic repression in Iran).

Givi Alkhazishvili · the celebrated Georgian poet died in August at the age of seventy-seven. He was known as an experimenter with different poetic forms and as a teacher of Georgian literature, writing about its traditions and about literature in translation. He also worked as an editor and publisher.

Michael Horovitz · *Colin Still writes*: I first encountered Michael Horovitz when I was in my teens, at a reading at St Pancras Town Hall, when he read alongside Christopher Logue and Lawrence Ferlinghetti. I was struck by his confident presence, his cultured accent, and (as I recall) his red velvet jacket. The poems were political, focused (again, as I recall) on issues like nuclear disarmament, though shot through with a Goon Show-like humour. As a souvenir of the event I bought a copy of a recently published issue of his magazine *New Departures*. This was the double issue, numbers 2/3, which featured the likes of Allen Ginsberg and Eugene Ionesco, but also names which were then unfamiliar to me, like John Cage, Raymond Queneau

and Robert Creeley: signposts, as it turned out, to directions which I'd follow for the rest of my life.

Michael William (Yechiel Ha-Levi) Horovitz was born in Frankfurt in 1936, the tenth child of orthodox Jewish parents, who fled to England when Michael was two. He was brought up in strict orthodoxy, which, to the despair of his father, he found increasingly antipathetic. 'I saw tears in his eyes,' he told me when I was filming him. 'He would say, in German, "You've got this quick understanding, you are so bright, and yet you're squandering it away. You just make fun, you're supposed to be serious". He was just desolated that any son of his should be so frivolous and superficial and secular.'

At eighteen, Michael went up to Oxford to read English. It was there that he developed what was to be a lifelong passion for jazz and began seriously to write poetry (though 'seriously' is perhaps the wrong word when it comes to Michael's writing). As a student he was particularly drawn to the work of William Blake, on which he had plans,

which he later abandoned, to write a PhD. After Oxford he returned to London, beginning what was to be a lifelong, hand-to-mouth, existence as a man of letters, putting his seemingly limitless energies into *New Departures*, which he founded in 1959, managing from the start to get contributions from such major figures as Jean Genet, Samuel Beckett and William Burroughs. In tandem with the magazine he ran Live New Departures, a series of often haphazard events involving poets, comedians and jazz musicians, among them the pianist Stan Tracey and the blues singer/lyricist Pete Brown, both of whom would perform with him for decades. It was Michael's delight to join the musicians on stage, playing his 'anglo-saxophone', a kazoo which he had modified with cardboard, cowhorn and gaffer tape to create an instrument reminiscent of the *shofar*, the ramshorn of Jewish ritual.

An event with which Michael was associated, and about which he was constantly being interviewed, was the International Poetry Incarnation, an all-star reading which took place at The Royal Albert Hall on 11 June 1965. Hastily organised, to take advantage of the presence in London of Allen Ginsberg, it proved to be a legendary event, attended by 7,000 people and featuring, among others, Ginsberg, Ferlinghetti, Christopher Logue, Andrei Voznesensky and Adrian Mitchell. Mitchell read 'To Whom It May Concern (Tell Me Lies About Vietnam)', and Michael a section of his anti-war poem 'For Modern Man'. The event was recorded by the film-maker Peter Whitehead, and released under the title 'Wholly Communion'.

In the years that followed Michael and Allen maintained a strong friendship. Something which they had in common was a love of William Blake, and each in his distinctive way began to sing Blake's *Songs of Innocence and Experience*, Michael with an ensemble which he called The William Blake Klezmatrix Band, a group which had at its core trombonist Annie Whitehead and keyboard player Peter Lemer, with Michael himself singing and performing on kazoo, one of their first public performances being in the Raphael Court at the Victoria and Albert Museum.

One of Michael's most attractive qualities was his almost infinite range of interests and his ability to recruit others, including in his endeavours the likes of Paul McCartney, Kylie Minogue, Lol Coxhill, Paul Weller, Damon Albarn, David Hockney, Peter Blake, John Hegley & the cellist Ayanna Witter-Johnson. Always one to promote the work of other people, Michael edited two important anthologies, *Children of Albion*, published by Penguin in 1969, and a second volume, *Grandchildren of Albion*. Though Michael liked to be regarded as a Beat writer and rejoiced in his links with Ginsberg, the scope of the anthologies, like that of Live New Departures, was remarkably catholic, featuring writers as diverse as Linton Kwesi Johnson, Edwin Morgan, Andrew Crozier, Sujata Bhatt, Billy Bragg and John Agard.

Whilst essentially a metropolitan figure – he spent most of his life in Notting Hill – he lived for some years in rural Gloucestershire, where he was married to the poet Frances Horovitz, mother of his son Adam, now an established poet. Recalling the years he spent with Frances, who died in 1983, Michael wrote an uncharacteristically lyrical rural elegy called *A Midsummer Morning's Jog Log*.

At the approach of the Millennium Michael produced a 464-page volume called *The New Wasteland*: *Timeship Earth at Nillennium*, a diatribe against the effects of the Thatcher years, the mendacity of the press, the failure of New Labour, the military interventions in the Middle East and, as he put it, 'the suicidal commercial triumphalism promoted by the arms, nuclear, advertising and war industries'. This passionately conceived volume, half of which was in the form of notes in support of its arguments, incorporated a great mass of artworks, political cartoons & newspaper articles, and was the result of an enormous amount of research. With good reason, Horovitz the Pacifist regarded this book, sprawling and uneven though it might seem, as his *magnum opus*.

Over the years he became increasingly recognised: he was awarded an OBE, in 2010 he contested the chair of Oxford Professor of Poetry, which he lost (perhaps as well) to Geoffrey Hill, and he was often to be heard on the radio, on programmes such as *Private Passions* and *Great Lives*, when he chose to discuss the life of Allen Ginsberg.

As he got older, Michael, never a conformist, became more and more eccentric. Dressed in 'flower power' shirts and wearing the floppy, rose-patterned peak cap that became his trademark, he could be seen at every event, dragging a pull-along case full of merchandise: his POP, POW, POM and POT anthologies, which he would as often as not give away free of charge. An inveterate hoarder, his flat became full of papers, not just his own archives, but old newspapers, magazines and flyers, stacked several feet high, with the result that to cross the room one had to negotiate a zigzag series of trench-like passages. Diabetic in later years, he nevertheless became the beneficiary of a local pastry cook who would supply him each day with unsold cream cakes, which for Michael became a kind of personal currency which he would pass on to his friends. A scarcely concealed secret was that it was Michael who, from time to time, contributed the appalling verses of E.J. Thribb (aged 17 ½) to *Private Eye*...

In 2012 his life took an unexpected turn when he formed a relationship with Vanessa Vie, a Spanish painter, singer and lyricist, almost forty years his junior. For a decade they performed together, with evident pleasure in each other's company, singing a combination of Blake songs and Vanessa's own playful words. This was a genuinely symbiotic relationship, on a personal as well as a musical level. Vanessa was a great source of support in Michael's later years, as his health declined. He died on 7 July, aged eighty-six. His funeral was held, on a scorchingly hot day, in Kensal Green Cemetery, a part secular, part religious event, attended by more than a hundred friends and fellow artists and conducted by a rabbi. Following spoken tributes by Michael's son Adam and by John Agard, Vanessa bade farewell to him, not with words, but with a protracted and achingly poignant lament, sounded, most appropriately, on Michael's kazoo, his *shofar*.

Reports

Sound Sutra: A Decade of Resonances

i.m. Colin Robinson

VAHNI CAPILDEO

1. An irresistible invitation is not what you may expect late at night during a working week in a pandemic. However, an irresistible invitation is what arrived. The poet Carrie Etter, sharing her draft novel-in-verse, *Exit Kassandra*, matter-of-factly mentioned: 'It reads aloud in 50 minutes.' Accordingly, I have been reading it aloud; but it took me three days, with intermissions. Why?

2. Midsummer has passed, and August approaches. August has resonance. Do not begin anything in the month that corresponds to August this year, I once was advised, because in this season Lord Vishnu is asleep, and you need the creative play of his energy. I imagined his whirling conch shell stilled, and Sesh Naag, the great serpent who serves as his throne, a peaceful heap of coils, slumbering on a blue ocean out of time, also stilled. The rhythm of sleep-breathing and the colour blue permeate 'August' ever since.

3. Thinking with anniversaries is human. Noting and reflecting on true anniversaries, the ones that call for a new or personal calendar, is hardly encouraged. Don't be morbid; don't cling! Why? Is it that people with the sense of weaving a whole cloth of life may be less amenable to being draped in a flag? We are more governable if we can be kept reactive in the instant, and useful for the task at hand. Replace milestones with official ceremonies, better yet with a squabble over commemoration. Clap and forget; click and collect. Interviewed by Alice Hiller, Shivanee Ramlochan says: "I came to understand this as my duty of care to the work: to not only present the future as viable, in the face of such shattering trauma, but to manifest the future as an active catalyst, the future as present and viable and full of agency'."

4. Unremembered anniversaries are not silent. They make themselves known by resonance. You might lose your temper with colleagues and – unlike a character in a Woolfian novel – fail to note that the blaze of apple blossom and the position of your foot on the stair have crystallized the same as when you heard the news of that death, that other time, in that other place. You might just feel thirsty, yet unable to pour yourself a glass of water.

5. 'Anniversary' is an unquiet word. Its etymology seems to desire confusion. It resembles *versare*, like something that pours itself out. It descends not from *versare*, but from *vertere*. It turns. It overthrows. Our cells are osmotic, and we are endangered by anniversaries, which are liquid; overthrow resembles overflow. 'Volt' is a similar word. Turning the metal tap in the candlelit bathroom during a thunderstorm, as a child, I stuck to the tap; lightning struck, and I was shocked. Flicking the bathroom light switch with damp fingers, this year, I snatched my hand away, shocking myself. Volts, delivered into my body, add themselves to how my memory processes the word 'volta'. My embodied experience of relating to the word, by association, makes the turn or break in any sonnet extra electric, even though I know the poetic craft term has not entered the language the same way as its distant, scientific kin, Alessandro Volta's surname.

6. Sputnik, the world's first artificial satellite, launched by the Soviet Union in 1957, gave rise to a set of words: beatnik, peacenik, refusenik: not really related to its 'fellow traveller' meaning. Beyond etymology, into emotion, doesn't the productive suffix -nik stamp these neologisms with a space-age flair? Is a productive suffix like a productive cough, bringing stuff up? Could -versary be a productive suffix? The unsparing, bloody, and redemptive poet Shivanee Ramlochan writes: 'On the Third Anniversary of the Rape'. Rapeversary. Deathiversary. Revengersary. Riseversary. Could these be words, too? They pour themselves into my mind. They walk. They turn.

7. Carrie Etter's *Exit Kassandra* took me three days to read out loud because its ancient world made anew

played out against an insurrectionversary, two grandpaternal deathiversaries, and one of my rapeversaries, all falling between late July and late August. This month is full of noises. Pay attention! Etter's tender, violated, copper-haired prophetess is brilliantly reconceived. Lines of broken-off sense but perfect syntax are presented as end-stopped. The form repeats, overlaps, and brings the story to completion like the spars of a ruined boat. They stick into the air, and our brain fills in the wartime shape that was prophesied.

8. Where does the sea of resonances take us next? Why not to Shakespeare, who writes that the sounds and sweet airs of the isle in the *Tempest* 'give delight, and hurt not'? Ah. Is he winking over the head of his savage character, whose name – Caliban – is remixed, to knowing hearers, into resonances of flesh-eating and foreignness? Carib, Caribal, Cannibal. When Ariel and Prospero send a sleep upon incomers, isn't this be the settler-colonial enjoyment of narrative control as refined magic, only self-deprecatingly dismissed as 'rough magic'? When Shelley writes 'Music, when soft voices die, Vibrates in the memory', he is both revolutionary and romantic. He nudges us towards attunement and awareness. He does not merely lull.

9. What is 'mere' (simple, not sea-like or lake-like; now, also, poured into those associations, mere, mare, marine) about lulling? I remember the horror of seeing a man recorded in the south of England rocking a mawmet, a witch-doll, and doing a 'humming spell', to make someone in the village leave, go away, leave, leave. His voice disturbed the air in a way that could be imagined rippling to the end of a village. I remember reading the real or fake news about Cuba, that beleaguered island up and to the left of us, while I was in Trinidad – about covert sonic weapons that damage the soft brain. 'Made my ears bleed' is not only a metaphor. I remember an 'Exiled Writers Ink' performance in London, when I felt guilty at my instinctual, or musicked, reaction to a Persian poet reciting in Persian. I understood almost no words and could not square how deeply I was (we are) moved by the force of pattern, the ferocity of presence.

Merely? Mere?

10. When the ferry 'The Island Discovery' was pitching during a blowy crossing from Inishbofin to Cleggan, Deirdre Ní Chonghaile picked up her fiddle and walked up and down, playing it. Her music gave shape to the present. Each phrase implied a shapely future, then brought about its promise. As she played, some people stopped vomiting. I put my head down. I had not been vomiting, but I was deeply sleepy. The movement of the sea and the vibrations in the air sent me peacefully under, till we were almost in port. Deirdre's figure inserts itself into the New Testament passages where Jesus is sleeping through a storm at sea, till his frightened disciples wake him. What is the Christian God doing in that passage? You can read the sea as representing the chaotic, the barely controlled, the doom that must be pushed back again and again. You can read coming to shore as passing through death and the waters of baptism to Easter and Resurrection. I like to read the sleep naturally: as an Edenic moment of oneness with nature. The disciplines, being attuned to mortality, and goal-oriented, were not (could not be) as open to the poetry of weather.

This string of associative meditations on resonance has been pieced together in memory of Colin Robinson, who died on March 4, 2021, at the age of 58. An exemplary activist for LGBT+ rights in the Caribbean, Colin was a gifted artist and writer. Calling out from the loneliness of terminal cancer during Trinidad and Tobago's high-surveillance lockdown, he brought together family and friends for a virtual session that that lacked the hugging and humming, the awkwardness and joy, of bodily togetherness, but was alive with reminiscence. Thanks to the Lloyd Best Institute of the Caribbean, we had Zoom power; from our many on-screen islands, many voices recited our most beloved verses by Colin, bringing them back to the author himself. His face, so full of power when we shared the stage, not long ago, as Midnight Robbers, was agleam, refined to the bones of community in joy. While loss remembers us, Colin's chief gift was always love. We can choose to live with his resonance.

Martyr's Memorial, The Death of the Traditional Wait

PATRICK McGUINNESS

Opposite the Broad Street entrance to Boswells, where they sell university-crested sweatshirts, caps, union jack cushions, Frank Cooper's 'Oxford' marmalade, etc., is a small ancient island amid the roar of traffic. It consists of a graveyard, a church, a monumental spire and underground women's toilets. The church and graveyard are surrounded by railings with tethered bikes. I pass them every day but have never been in. Today that changes. It's a High Church place, ancient of course like so much else around here, and it smells of incense. In the 10th C, it was on the outside of Oxford city walls – the North Gate being on Cornmarket in the old Oxford. It's an impressive place, restored in 1842 by the young Gilbert Scott. It has famous bells, and in an Inspector Morse novel, Morse's love interest is a bell-ringer and church caretaker. Morse's love interest always fails, either through his failure of nerve or because she turns out to be the *who* that *dunnit*. Spoiler alert: in this Morse, it's the latter.

Behind the church is The Martyr's Memorial, to the protestant victims of Queen Mary: Cranmer, Latimer and Ridley. They were burned close by, just outside the city walls, and a cross in the tarmac of Broad Street marks the spot. But here is where they are remembered, though not by any of the people who sit and drink there. Not by me much of the time either. That's the thing about memorials – few people remember them and even fewer notice them. The monument was designed by Gilbert Scott three hundred years after they were burned, and looks like the steeple of a Gothic church that sank underground. The three martyrs are sculpted on the sides, serenely at prayer. Beneath them, it's less serene. Mornings and daytime, it's drinkers, often with dogs; in the afternoons and evenings, it's language school students. In the old days they had ghetto blasters, but now it's iPods with bluetooth connections to minuscule but powerful speakers. Tourists rest here, consulting apps and maps.

In the days before mobile phones, we'd meet here from all corners of the city before deciding where to go. Technology has killed that species of place, and that species of time, where hanging about happened: intermediate zones and intermediate durations, always on the way to somewhere else, to some other moment, to what we called 'events'. Waiting is different now; it's a mishap or an obstacle rather than a routine or a condition. Oxford is full of places I used to wait at or in which I now pass, destination-fixated because all my arrangements are being made in 'real' time. What other time is there? (Well, lots, but that's a different story.) I've forgotten most of these meeting-places, but I remember this one because this is where I'd wait for my faculty to open – the Taylor Institution on the other side of the road – so I could give my 9 a.m. lectures on *Waiting for Godot*. In true method-acting style, I'd do different kinds of waiting in order to show that the play, and what it conveyed,

was first of all rooted in experience, in how we live. Only then did it start to have abstract things like symbolism. I'd ask volunteers from the audience to demonstrate the difference between waiting and waiting *for*, and I think they learned more from doing that than from my academic books.

In 1995 I organised a poetry reading and invited Donald Davie, who read in St John's with Seamus Heaney and James Fenton. Davie informed me by letter that he wanted to meet at the Martyrs' Memorial so I waited here, phoneless and expectant. I thought it was just a convenient meeting-point, but for him it was more. He put down his bags and bowed his head. A staunch protestant footsoldier, Davie talked about them as if we could still smell the burning. I make him sound fierce and maybe he was, but I was an atheist and I spent quite a large part of my twenties trying to be the sort of person I wasn't in order to measure up to him. He was kind to me and encouraged me when there was no need to. I admired his work, and cared about him deeply. He read that night with amazing power. It was August, hot and sticky. I didn't know it but he was dying. I was due to visit him in late September, but he died the week before in that unexpected-expected way of cancer sufferers. I sit on the steps of the Martyrs' Memorial and have a memorial wait. I've brought the copy of *To Scorch of Freeze* he gave me – his reading copy, with his little annotations, references, anecdote-prompts. Of all the poems of his I've loved and thought about, these are the lines I read out now:

> 'Do you believe in a God
> who can change the course of events
> on earth?'
> 'No, just
> the ordinary one'.
>
> A laugh,
> but not so stupid: events
> He does not, it seems, determine
> for the most part. Whether He could
> is not to the point; it is not
> stupid to believe in
> a God who mostly abjures.

It's not so different from Godot, and the 'God who mostly abjures' is the kind of God I could imagine.

Beside me now are some people eating supermarket sushi, and two men, on the cusp of what the law used to define as vagrancy, sharing a 4 pack of cider. One of them has the last can, which still has the four plastic rings attached, 'yokes' they're called in the drinks trade, so that whenever he takes a sip he seems to be looking out through enormous spectacles. I'm sure the cider will help with that effect.

Releasing the Sparks

JONATHAN SIMONS

As more of our lives are swept up and digitised by vast corporate networks of spectacle, ours may be the last generation with one foot still touching down in the analog world. We may be the last to have come of age under the influence of such old-world obstacles as boredom, solitude, and silence. Every generation has its share of vices, though none as accessible and spellbinding as the Internet, connecting us without pause to the gossip and chatter of three billion other users. Even before this dreadful pandemic came and pushed us deeper into the web, we were already hooked. The question we face now is whether there will remain enough of us who value the authenticity of local creative communities.

To digital natives, our analog upbringing seems like an unbearable wasteland. Just the idea of running out of entertainment, spending entire afternoons daydreaming, alone and unreachable, baffles and unsettles them. Yet the genesis of any creative revolution depends upon leisure, upon having enough time, space, and autonomy – what we used to call privacy – to develop vital capacities to think, to feel, and to dream.

From the rubble of our barbarity, we do manage, on occasion, to build thriving civilizations. When the underlying conditions are ripe and a community garners enough solidarity and vision to lift itself up from the debris of history, it's artists and philosophers we most often find leading the way.

It's not a matter of glorifying bygone eras; we've always been animals. The urge to support offline culture in the digital age isn't nostalgia but rather an acknowledgement that the Internet, despite appearances, is not actually a living thing. In fact, there are many critical differences between *virtual* reality and a life lived through all of the senses. What kind of torture would strip a person entirely of smell, texture, and taste? And when you then take away physical affection, skin and touch, and the shared vulnerability of shared space, relationships stagnate and become convincing approximations, reminiscent of the plastic smiles of models gleaming down at us from advertising billboards.

The digital age engenders the most peculiar doubts, such as whether words on a screen are the same as words on a page, whether posting a photograph of a mountain is more or less compelling than climbing it, whether the menu itself is the meal, whether a text message can feel as erotic as a kiss. We ponder such questions while leaning out from our fragile precipice of physicality, peering down at the new landscapes, vast and effervescent, ensconced in flickering blue light. We discover a world where human touch and eye contact are increasingly mediated by glass control panels.

After two hundred years of machines ripping nature to pieces, and then twenty years perfecting a suitably disembodied sham reality, how will we ever manage to rescue a planet we now only glimpse through our screens? The answer to this question is piped in these days like an anthem: more and better technology will save us.

The new technologies indeed give us tremendous power but also deplete our lives of reverie and leisure. Our curiosities are too quickly quenched or sidelined. There is little time or space for thoughts to linger, to coalesce, to become drumbeats of longing or visionary calls for a saner world. What is the value of finding something when we no longer have the luxury of being lost? What happens when the shadow of the rose appears livelier than the rose itself, when the mirage dazzles us more than the desert, when the replica replaces the real?

In the digital age, fragmentation gives way to atrophy, to numbness, until the purpose of adulthood is relegated to little more than the relentless pursuit of mastery over the mundane. But as children, we knew that life was a treasure hunt. We knew that trees were growing limbs for us to climb. We were mesmerised by the power of our own sustained attention, and we knew how to release the sparks.

Letter from Wales

SAM ADAMS

I have been browsing James Keery's *Apocalypse* – a big and bold collection of the 'visionary modernist' poetry that came rapidly to the boil in the 1930s and '40s, simmered through middle of the last century and spilled over in splashes during a decade or so beyond. It promises food for the mind extending far into the future. Understandably, I hope, I turned first to familiar names, in whose company it has felt much like old times: the same whirling imagery and (often enough) the same bafflement. But what's poetry for, if not to make us think?

Keery acknowledges, with the minutest hesitation, that 'the central body of work is that of Dylan Thomas'. Well, there's a connection for a start: Thomas's explosive entry into the literary world, *18 Poems*, saw the light of day in December 1934, a few weeks after I did, and I was lucky enough to catch up with him at Aberystwyth in 1952, when, single-handed, he held a packed student audience enthralled. I do not exaggerate: I have attended many poetry readings since, some very fine and special, but none to compare with that evening in Aber.

One or two reviewers saw in Thomas's early published poetry the taint of surrealism, which they did not much care for. Tackled on the subject later, he forswore any influence or indeed knowledge of the movement. This was a fib. During the International Surrealist Exhibition at the New Burlington Galleries, June–July 1936, he had carried a cup of boiled string around asking visitors whether they would like it weak or strong. In the introduction and notes to his 'New Centenary Edition' of Thomas's *Collected Poems* (2014), John Goodby argues convincingly that the poet's choice of word and image was conscious rather than generated in the surrealist unconscious, and reveals the multi-layered complexity of imagery and technical virtuosity displayed in poems selected by Keery: 'Before I knocked and flesh let enter', and 'The force that through the green fuse drives the flower', both products of his teenage years. 'The Rimbaud of Cwmdonkin Drive' indeed! I am reminded of Patrick McGuinness's observation that the only way Thomas's apocalyptic poetry can meaningfully be compared with the French poet's equally youthful *oeuvre* is in being precise even when it is incomprehensible.

By my count the anthology includes another fourteen Welsh poets, from David Jones (1895–1974) to Daniel Huws (born 1932), plus George Woodcock, a Canadian with a Welsh aunt, who was gathered into Keidrych Rhys's 1944 Faber anthology *Modern Welsh Poetry*, together with Henry Treece, whose half-Welsh parentage may reveal itself in 'the slag heap and steam-organ town' ('Song for an Ending') in Keery's selection, and Robert Herring, who, in his brief offering, supplies the apt phrase 'first flames of the apocalypse' and, with no discernible Welsh connection, brought out no fewer than five Welsh numbers of *Life and Letters To-day*. (There is a splendid account of the creative interaction between

Herring and Welsh writers of the 1930s and '40s, and much more beside, in Meic Stephens' article 'The Third Man: Robert Herring and Life and Letters To-day' in *Welsh Writing in English*, Vol. 3, 1997.)

Apocalypse has two 'Sonnets of the Madonna' by John Ormond from *Life and Letters To-day* that reveal with stunning clarity the profound effect Dylan had on gifted younger poets. Ormond (or Ormond Thomas as he was at that time) heeded Vernon Watkins' advice not to publish any more poems until he was thirty. In consequence, he destroyed a lot of work, and the sonnets do not appear in the *Collected Poems* edited by his daughter Rian Evans.

The title of R.S. Thomas's 'Maes-yr-Onnen' means 'ash-tree field', but refers to the three-hundred-year-old chapel on an anciently gifted field in Radnorshire of particular significance in nonconformism: it was the first Congregational meeting house in Wales. This is the repository of 'stale piety' the Anglican cleric and dedicated twitcher is describing on a fair, blue, breezy day, though the twittering in the rafters that so surprised and delighted him he ascribes to 'Rhiannon's birds', those creatures of magic in *The Mabinogion* the giant Ysbaddaden demands for the hand of his daughter, Olwen, in marriage to Culhwch, which (in Sioned Davies's Oxford translation, 2007) have the power to 'wake the dead and lull the living to sleep'.

Keidrych Rhys's magazine, *Wales,* published many of those recruited to *Apocalypse.* Vernon Watkins and Dylan Thomas were close friends and frequent correspondents. Thomas, wearing a suit borrowed from Watkins, was best man at Rhys's wedding to Lynette Roberts, a poet of assured apocalyptic status. Among the couple's visitors at Llanybri in Carmarthenshire, were R.S. Thomas, Alun Lewis and Glyn Jones. Although temperamentally unlike, Dylan and Glyn Jones were friends: Jones was probably at the Surrealist Exhibition with Thomas. John Ormond and Dylan Thomas were friends; Ormond, with Daniel Jones, brought Thomas's body back from Southampton for burial. Alun Lewis and Brenda Chamberlain, with her husband, the artist John Petts, collaborated in producing *The Caseg Broadsheets* – and so on. Few in the entire list were not subjected to the scrupulous analysis of Roland Mathias in books, articles and reviews. It's almost as though all were neighbours in one terraced street, dropping in on one another, taking tea together, talking over the garden wall.

Glyn Jones's contribution to the anthology is unique. His work appears twice, once under his own name, once, with the poem 'Perfect', in the guise of 'Hugh MacDiarmid'. Keery presents this phenomenon as an example of 'interfluentiality':

I found a pigeon's skull on the machair,
All the bones pure white and dry, and chalky,

But perfect,
Without a crack or a flaw anywhere.

At the back, rising out of the beak,
Were twin domes like bubbles of thin bone,
Almost transparent, where the brain had been
That fixed the tilt of the wings.

The first line alone is MacDiarmid's, the remainder taken verbatim from Glyn Jones's story 'Porth-y-Rhyd'. In the story, which, if prose were admitted, would stand as a fine example of apocalyptic writing, the description of the skull (it is a seagull's) continues ' ... wings, with the contour of delicate sutures inked in a crinkled line across the skull, and where the brow-bone sloped down into the beak were two dark holes like goggles ... and lacing the weight of the beak upward to the skull were struts of slender bone, long and delicate, and taut as a hawser ...' It is tempting to continue MacDiarmid's find, amplify his poem, to end with the striking image of bones 'long and delicate, and taut as a hawser'. With acknowledgement to both Glyn Jones and MacDiarmid, would it then be my poem?

'Perfect' was published, and reprinted, without reference to its source, though Keery makes clear it is a 'found' poem, and the story of where exactly MacDiarmid found it has long been known. It is told in Tony Brown's excellent *The Collected Stories of Glyn Jones* (UWP 1999), while the fullest account is again supplied by Meic Stephens, in the *New Welsh Review* No. 23 (Winter 1993–94). Suffice it to say Glyn Jones was very annoyed about the affair, and took action through his agent. I met Hugh MacDiarmid, briefly, at Meic's home in Cardiff in April 1974. Later the same day, Meic invited Glyn and his wife Doreen to dinner, where they were introduced to Christopher Grieve and Valda. The poets sat together on a sofa, one with a whisky, the other an orange juice, and agreeing, by that time anyway, there no embarrassment on either side, 'engaged in an animated, wide-ranging conversation about books and writers'.

Brian Johnstone

ROBYN MARSACK

Brian Johnstone, poet and co-founder of StAnza – Scotland's international poetry festival – died in May, a month after the online launch of what he knew would be his last collection, *The Marks on the Map*.

In his memoir *Double Exposure* (2017) Brian described his genteel upbringing in Edinburgh, where he was born in 1950. His mother thought plain loaves, listening to music on a 'transistor radio' and Glasgow were 'common'. Brian, however, relished the changes the 1960s and 1970s offered in Scotland. His old friend Drew Clegg recalled the heady days of undergraduate life in St Andrews, when Brian was the Entertainments Convenor and persuaded Pink Floyd to come to the town. 'Back then you might have seen the Floyd in London at the Roundhouse or in Paris or Berlin, but St Andrews? Brian charmed them and they came and in that youthful moment,' Drew wrote in his tribute on the StAnza blog, 'we can see the quintessential Brian Johnstone. You aim high.' Brian celebrated music 'from Elvis to Ivan, from Dusty to Sandy, from Beatles to Incredibles, from Skiffle to Prog' in his 2018 pamphlet *Juke Box Jeopardy*, handsomely published by Red Squirrel.

While working as a primary-school teacher in Edinburgh, Brian lapsed from writing for a long period, but after he founded Shore Poets with Roz Brackenbury in 1991, he returned to a serious pursuit of poetry. Scottish Cultural Press published his first full collection, *The Lizard Silence*, in 1996. Shore Poets, shortly to celebrate its 30th anniversary, mixed established and new voices in the convivial atmosphere that Brian was so adept at creating, combining poetry, music and a café style.

The end of the decade returned him to St Andrews, where with his co-founders Gavin Bowd and Anna Crowe, he set up StAnza, of which he was Festival Director until 2010. Anna paid this tribute:

It was my pleasure and privilege to work alongside him in planning a new Scottish poetry festival. From the very beginning Brian, who had a lot of experience in organising poetry readings throughout Fife, had ambitious hopes for what has become StAnza (the cunningly-spelled title was his idea). We were keen to make the festival international in scope, and Brian had the vision and energy to see how this could be achieved. He saw immediately that it would be crucial to the festival's success to involve the newly rebuilt Byre Theatre, and to make it our hub, and he used his gifts of persuasion to convince the theatre management of this new idea, namely that poetry would in fact bring big audiences. Following advice to make the festival independent of the University, we were able to attract our own funding, and Brian had a tremendous gift for persuading people to back the festival.[...]

Brian was a man of great generosity and human warmth, with a gift for making friends. With his artist wife, Jean, he welcomed many visiting poets to their house in the Fife countryside. He was a dedicated poet with a distinctive, often melancholy voice and a passion for memorialising what others might overlook. His interest in music and art led him into fruitful collaboration. Brian will always be remembered as the man who made StAnza happen.

Having mentored his successor Eleanor Livingstone, Brian was a notable presence at every festival, with his signature white moustache and genial demeanour, Jean always at his side. They formed a habit of retreating to Crete to read, walk, and renew their artistic practice. He continued to be active in the poetry community, here and abroad, and found a steady publisher in Todmorden-based Arc. Angela Jarman wrote on Arc's blog:

Brian was the sort of poet that every publisher hopes to work with – engaging, uncompromisingly honest and thought provoking, yet reader-friendly and altogether entertaining. We have published three collections by him and always enjoyed the whole process, from receipt of the first draft of the manuscript to publication. He will be greatly missed.

His latest collection may be his strongest, some think; all the more reason to lament his death (from cancer). Two of his nurses had been his pupils, as it turned out, and recalled his being an inspirational teacher. 'A Lock of Fleece' from *The Marks on the Map* was read at his funeral. The title of the collection seems entirely appropriate for Brian, who did indeed make his mark on the poetry and cultural map of Scotland.

A lock of fleece
held tightly in the hand
when laid between the boards

enough to say this man
was never one to turn his face
away from God, say -

*Look, a shepherd comes
to hills he only could imagine.
Now let him pass.*

Winter Cadae

JOHN FULLER

1.
In winter
We
Are near freezing

Both

In body and mind,
But the thought of cycles consoles us.
A verse
Like this tries to rehearse

The formula, thus:

Unconfined
Ratio of growth
In the yearly return of Spring;
Periphery of Persephone/
Diameter, Demeter.

2.
Pale moon, our
Friend,
How you coldly

Stare

From your battlements
At our blood and tides, without concern,
And throw

Light wherever you go

That's not yours to burn!

There's no sense
In that haughty air
Of self-possession, don't you see?
It reflects badly on you to send
Back such light hour after hour.

3.
How I wish
That
We were walking

By

The retreating tide,
Stumbling over clumped laver on to
Clear sand,
Finding round sea-shells and

Look! some shapes quite new,

That have died
Not wishing to die
In the moon's cruel marooning:
Rings of glittering crushed goblets that
Turn out to be jellyfish.

4.
As the gulls
Stir
The lifting air

And

Howl down the black seas
As though the night tide made them less free
And as
Sky and ocean compass

Their circles, so the

Moon-jellies
On the endless sand
Look round as well, and everywhere
Turned yet unturned pebbles. No wonder:
Nature abhors right angles.

5.
Favoured ground:
I
Stand at a loss

Here

In the wintry light,
With the loaf-loving ducks in full voice,
The pond
Something to get beyond

That offers a choice:

Left or right?
The answer is clear.
No water can be walked across.
How much longer does it take? Ask pi,
I think, as I walk around.

6.
As you were:
Thumb
Between your lips

In

Babyish pleasure
Or scratch-scratch in pursuit of something
So true

That there's nothing to do

But go on waiting.

On cue, your
Doubts start flooding in,
Regular as the moon's eclipse.
Fullness of knowledge can never come.
It's an infinite number.

7.
Admire the
Blood's
Circulation:

Hour

By hour, minute by
Minute, second by second, it moves
Toward
The heart and is restored.

Its vigour improves:

By-and-by
The lungs give it power
And it is rich with oxygen,
Flows along the arteries and floods
The body with energy.

8.
Can you tell
Me
Something of love?

It

Is that notional
And elusive centre of our sphere
Which brings
Us from our wanderings

Back to what is dear

To us all,
Since its opposite
Kills us, when clouds gather above
The horizons of exploit and the
Challenging circles of hell.

9.
As a boy
I
Was always struck

By

The strange constancy
Of ratios, when *a* divides *b*,
Each time
Just the same, like a rhyme.

Now in age I see

What would be
Close enough to pi:
My days by occasions of luck,
My nights by indicative dreams, my
Whole life divided by joy.

10.
We prefer
The
Bright sense of eyes.

Why

Do diameters
Always relate to circumference?
The robe
Of light drenches the globe

In magnificence.

Our sight stirs
Within radii
Which, paired and opposed, define size,
An inwardness of scope, but singly
Will radiate for ever.

11.
Time is in
Name
And in nature

A

Sharpster who likes to
Play with moons and tides and ice and suns

And seeks
To mark the pack of weeks

Whose suits are seasons

And cheat you,
However you play,
Of all your hope and composure.
Time holds all the cards. It's a long game
You know you can never win.

12.
All too soon
Wide
Arcs of distress

Split

Our world apart, take
Us off balance; whereas all we need
Is that
Sense of proceeding at

A suitable speed

Where we make
What we make of it,
Calmly channelling, more or less
Like a conduit, inside and outside,
Tides of the heart and the moon.

13.
Our failing
Star
Draws all round it

In

Endless curvature
And (at a terrifying distance)
What we
Hope is consistency,

And though all is chance

We endure,
As they turn and spin,
These hands of the hour and minute,
That empty page in the calendar,
The painful return of Spring.

14.
Finely
We
Know what we want,

Though

It's impossible.
We want to say 'Not Yet' for ever.
We say

It as a kind of play

With our shared pulse, a

Tidal pull
Where moon-jellies go,
Their circumferences still cont-
racting and expanding beneath the
Moonlit waters, silently.

Thom Gunn Letters

COLM TÓIBÍN

The Letters of Thom Gunn, edited by Michael Nott, August Kleinzahler and Clive Wilmer (Faber) £40

Even his name was a work in progress. On a facsimile of the first folio text of 'Julius Caesar', he signed himself Thomson William Gunn and added the date, October 1944, which means he was fifteen. On the first page of his copy of 'The Poems of Alfred Tennyson 1830–1863', he signed his name T.W. Gunn and gave the address as Covey Hall, Snodland, Kent, the house where he and his brother lived after their mother's suicide in December 1944. In August 1947, when he was seventeen, he signed his name a simple Tom Gunn on the first page of his copy of 'The British Drama'.

His sexual identity, in these early years, was also open to suggestion. John Lehmann was the first editor outside Cambridge to take anything he had written. In his short essay in tribute to Lehmann, Gunn admitted that he had 'conveniently blocked...from memory' what they spoke about in 1954 when they met for the first time. But Lehmann remembered. In the middle of talk about poetry, it seems, Gunn blurted out 'that being published nationally didn't mean that I was going to have anything to do with *London homosexuals*.' When Lehmann, who was homosexual, reminded him of this, Gunn wondered: 'And what *did* I want or mean by it... I who surely knew what I was about sexually by this time, in fact going about everywhere with my lover?'

Lehmann would not, Gunn added, have recognized the remark about London homosexuals 'as a current tag from the followers of Leavis', F.R. Leavis being one of Gunn's teachers at Cambridge. 'Oh dear,' he adds, 'these were curious times and I was a curious person.'

As these letters make clear, Gunn came in many guises. At one moment, he is all drift and easy-going charm; at other times, he is filled with determination. He can be dogmatic, especially about poetry, but he can also be open-minded, ready to learn.

He was susceptible to influence – Leavis put a certain steel into Gunn's soul that appears right through his correspondence. Yvor Winters's eccentric and often intemperate views on poetry were taken up by Gunn, who studied with him at Stanford, at least for a while. Winters' method of creating his own canon, extolling a chosen few, disliking much of what was in fashion, also made its way into Gunn's judgements. (Twenty years after Winters' death, Gunn wrote: 'He has given me a strength which I do not in fact have – it is borrowed.' Gunn was proud that he had written poems about both Winters ('persistent, tough in will') and Robert Duncan ('whose great dread / Was closure'), whose influence nudged Gunn, who knew him in California, to loosen his strict use of metre and rhyme.

These were his surrogate fathers. The real one, a journalist in London, came to him in a dream in 1968, recounted to Tony Tanner, 'where I found my mother dead. I thought callously, "Oh no, not *again* [underlined]. I think I'll let somebody else find her body this time." Which I did! Also in this dream I got on very well with my father.'

In 1955, he wrote to his brother Ander: 'you can count me in on parricide.' Three years later, he wrote to a friend: 'Have you come across the Daily Sketch yet? (the world's most unscrupulous newspaper) My father is editor of it.' Four years later, he wrote to Robert Conquest: 'My father died recently, and I was rather shocked that I couldn't feel anything at all. I'd half expected I might feel something in spite of the fact that I'd never had much to do with him and he was, finally, a ruthless and self-pitying man.'

In 1976, he wrote of his stepmother: 'she eats boys and

girls live for breakfast every day.' When she died in 1991, he wrote to his aunts, his mother's sisters: 'Ander wrote me to that Olive died last December. Unpleasant man that I am, I let out a whoop of delight. One less hard, cynical, unloving bastard in the world. (Hell would be too kind to her.)'

Almost a decade later, he wrote to his aunts: 'You were very generous and kind to me in my teens. I often think of how disruptive I must have been to your lives in the 1940s, and I count myself lucky to have aunts who took me in so selflessly. Orphans are always a bore – but particularly in their teens.'

In California, where he went in 1954, Gunn gradually created a replacement family. When he and Mike Kitay, whom he had first met in Cambridge at the end of 1952, split up as lovers, they stayed housemates, being joined by Mike's lover Bill, and then by a couple of other gay men. In 1971, Gunn wrote to Tony Tanner: 'I have been (not unconsciously) idealizing the situation when I was a child after Father left home – I must have found the household of my mother and Ander and me very comfortable, so comfortable in fact that I have succeeded in reconstructing it now – Mike as my mother, Bill as my younger brother.'

In 'Lines for a Book', included in *The Sense of Movement* (1957), Gunn wrote a parody of Stephen Spender's poems:

'I think continually of those who were truly great':
'I think of all the toughs through history
And thank heavens they lived, continually.
I praise the overdogs from Alexander
To those who would not play with Stephen Spender.'

Once in America, Gunn became an overdog, a tough boy. In 1984, as he plans a curriculum, he writes: 'No Merrill or any other poet who admits going to the opera.' Eight years later, he writes of J.D. McClatchy: 'I am not one of his school (poets who write elegantly about opera).'

Instead, he liked the Beatles, the Stones, the Grateful Dead, Jefferson Airplane, and Crosby, Stills and Nash, whose single 'Suite: Judy Blue Eyes' he thought 'a fantastic sound. Beautiful. Best thing since The Band.' And he liked leather and motorbikes. It was as though he had taken Leavis's dislike of 'London homosexuals' to heart, and carried some of Leavis's rigour and toughness with him as he created a new identity. ('I have an awful tendency to transform sexual attraction into a moral value,' he wrote to his friend Tony White in 1955.

In that same letter, he described his first motorbike as 'positively sexually beautiful to look at... It is like bringing up a child, it constantly does things that surprise me...By the way, did you like On the Move, because I think that is better than anything else I have ever done.'

The second stanza of 'On the Move' begins, 'On motorcycles, up the road, they come:/Small, black, as flies hanging in heat, the Boys'... This set a tone that Gunn would pursue in ways both hot and cold. He liked will ('Much that is natural, to the will must yield') and he took a huge interest in boys. He liked energy; he enjoyed working in tones that were ostensibly impersonal but contained coiled emotions and desires. As a poet, he stood back and watched.

He also like the idea of pose ('Even in bed I pose,' his poem 'Carnal Knowledge' begins). He wrote further to Tony White about his motorbike: 'I know it's something of a pose (even more in the U.S. than in England), but what else can one do? One can to a certain extent be what one wants to be, and though doing this may start as a pose (and finish as one, if one's no good), there's a chance of its becoming the real thing.'

To another correspondent in 1955, he wrote: 'My motorcycle is wonderful. Did you see The Wild One?... Well, motorcycles are considered disreputable over here – only hoodlums ride them – and it is considered ODD for a teacher to ride one. This does much to help me feel at home in the university.'

In another letter, three years later, he wrote of motorcycles: 'The mere riding of one is, in a strange way, a sort of controlled irresponsibility.' While he gives the impression in some letters of enjoying total chaos and taking pure, irresponsible, hedonistic pleasure in the world, there was a side of Gunn that was in control. In later years, for example, when he was teaching semesters at Berkeley, he was not one of those stoned professors who let it all hang out. Gunn made clear to correspondents that this work engaged him fully; he postponed social encounters and drug taking until his teaching was done.

He took work seriously, but he wasn't proud of that. In 1955, he wrote to Tony White: 'Not doing anything makes me morose, ungrateful, arrogant, difficult to live with, etc. (Whereas working hard makes me morose, ungrateful, arrogant, and difficult to live with.)'

Sometimes, his interest in pose made him less than sensible. In 1960, he writes: 'I have got some German motorcycle boots.' And a week later, to Tony White: 'I'm trying to get a Nazi belt for this friend of mine in Calif., but can't find any nowadays. Where did you get yours and mine in England?' In an earlier letter to White, he writes about the concept of will. It 'is what distinguishes the existentialist from the Romantic. That would be the fine thing, for a man to be entirely will, with no emotions left. It leads to death, but a fine death.'

He has it in for England. In 1957, he wrote to Donald Hall: 'I find it difficult to know why I feel this complicated dislike of England, which is absolutely unreasoned.' When he heard that Allen Ginsberg, whom he would later admire, was being feted in England, he wrote to Robert Conquest: '*Howl* (underlined) (apart from being nonsense) is a mere catalogue, as bad as bad Whitman (who is always bad, anyway). I must say England has gone to the dogs – first Suez, now falling for Ginsberg.'

And then there is Larkin. In 1954, he wrote to Karl Miller about Larkin: 'The more I read him the more good I think him. He's fifteen times as good as me.' By 1956, he seems to have changed his mind. He wrote to Tony White: 'The fact that one's forced to say Philip Larkin is the best poet of our generation is quite shaking; he's a nice, quiet poet, but of no particular importance after all.' In 1977, he wrote of Larkin's readers: 'Most of those readers don't like L for the beauty of his form (although that is what I mainly like about him) – so what do they find attractive about his most prominent attitudes – his closed mind, his sour & begrudging tone, his assumption that provinciality is a virtue?' Twelve years later, after Larkin's death, he wrote: 'I have grouched about Larkin in the 70th issue of the PN Review, and grouched too much no doubt: I think that he is an exquisite poet, stylistically far better than Ted or me, for example, but disastrously limited by his choice of subject-matter – finally that choice has the effect of a kind of cowardice.'

The editors of Gunn's letters have included a large number of letters to a few close friends, most notably Tony White, actor and free spirit, also Tony Tanner and Douglas Chambers, both critics. This gives the book an intensity, a sense of focus. With all three Gunn can write about his personal life as much as about his poetry. He can make jokes and be silly. And he can also be dead serious.

For example, in a letter to Tony White in 1955, clearly in reply to some comments on his poem 'On the Move', Gunn defends 'every stanza' of the poem. 'They are all necessary.' He points out that, while 'dust' and 'thunder' in the first stanza 'are general', they 'are given particular reference in the second, where they are repeated.' He tells White that he needs the first stanza because the poem 'is also about "one" (presumably me, or anyone) standing on the edge of a Californian highway and seeing [the motorcyclists] go past.'

If the fourth stanza of the poem generalizes, he writes, 'that's tough. There's nothing wrong with generalization in itself, so long as it is not vague. To generalize, one doesn't have to be either Augustan, or like Eliot (where every abstraction is a groan).'

Almost twenty years later, in a letter to White, he has other matters to contemplate: 'San Francisco continues absolutely outrageous. Imagine a huge old dosshouse converted into a "bath house", and you go in there especially on a Saturday night and there are at least 300 men in towels, all so laid back in drugs they can hardly stagger. And on holiday weekends, they are served "mescalin punch."'

To Douglas Chambers, he wrote about his reading of Heaney's 'Station Island', 'the best thing SH has done, I think', providing a striking insight into the tone of the poem: 'The whole thing is haunted – not by Dante, as is Heaney's intention, but by Dante through Eliot, which I assume is unintentional. The influence especially is of the blitz ghost appearing in imitation terza rima in Little Gidding, one of the few passages in TSE that I really love. From that passage Heaney borrows a whole general tone and feeling, besides many stylistic characteristics.'

In 1969, Gunn wrote to Tony Tanner about dropping acid in a place called Kirby's Cove. 'I knew it would be the best trip ever, as it was. There were about 40 people there, some girls, at least one married couple, and everyone dropped and everyone went naked until it got too cold. I can't describe how beautiful it all was...a feeling of discovery + a feeling of adequacy and delight in things discovered.'

The footnote to this directs us to Gunn's poem 'Grasses'. It helps to know that the world was being observed here by someone on acid:

Each dulling-green, keen, streaky blade of grass
Leans to one body when the breezes start:
A one-time pathway flickers as they pass,

Where paler toward the root the quick ranks part.

Three years later, Gunn wrote again to Tanner: 'I've been doing a lot of nice acid this year...I particularly like doing it around gay bars on a Saturday night. At the end of the trip you feel that as though you have an *epic (underlined)* behind you, the evening has been so crammed with incident and heroic action.'

He moved with equal passion from epic trips to the business of poetry. (In 1993 he wrote to Douglas Chambers: 'I hope I never have to choose between having an imagination and having a cock, the two work so well together, rather like the two horses of the soul in Plato.'

In 1955 he wrote to Tony White about changing a line for the sake of metre. 'You see I'm foreswearing that phoney appearance of sincerity I had from being almost unscannable.' Ten years later, when John Lehmann wished that Gunn 'didn't pull my poetry-making self so far away from my life-enjoying sense', Gunn agrees that 'one of my troubles...is in not being able to get down on paper the whole of what I find valuable or true about what I experience. I have a great delight in the trivial and casual – things one may see on the street...But I have not yet found a good framework for these – the mere recording of them would not be very impressive.'

In Part III of 'The Man with Night Sweats' (1992), however, Gunn attempted to find a framework for what he saw on the street in poems like 'Skateboard', 'Well Dennis O'Grady' and 'Outside the Diner'. In 1987, he wrote: 'I suspect that I have been trying to get into my poetry a lot of little stories and anecdotes that most people would put into short stories and novels and essays nowadays.'

The tone in his poems became relaxed, then tightened, then relaxed even more. Like a vengeful, insistent angel, Yvor Winters looked over his shoulder. In 1966, two years before Winters' death, his old teacher wrote to him: 'Your dissipated adventure in syllabics (or something) has weakened the whole texture of your perceptions. Your rhythms, when I can find them, are uninteresting; the diction is genteel but unimportant. I cannot remember the poems; they blur into each other and into nothing...You simply approach polite journalism.'

Gunn replied to say that Winters was 'probably right' and went on: 'I have decided to give up free verse (I gave up syllabics two years ago), since I don't seem to be doing very well with it, and am going back to meter. But I expect the period in retraining in meter to take some time!'

When Donald Davie sent Gunn his own version of Gunn's 'Last Days in Teddington', where he 'loosened the meter up a bit', Gunn thought the poem was now 'sloppy.' This led him to conclude that 'the rhythmic intention' of a poem 'has to be decided on very early.' One can, he wrote, 'make minor changes of rhythm, one can make such large changes as adding a stanza or deleting half the poem...but the rhythmic character of the poem is not something that can be changed like a piece of clothing.'

Just as he took on the guise of sexual tough guy, self-deprecating poet became another of his poses: 'I have been reading the proofs of my collected poems, 500 pages of them, TWICE, looking for errors and all I have been able to see in forty years of poetry is pretentiousness, datedness, and boredom, boredom, boredom...[I] felt about as kindly to the poetry in front of me as I were Ian Hamilton.' As we know from earlier letters, Gunn does not think much of Ian Hamilton.

Gunn's judgements of other poets can be harsh and dismissive, or else he overpraises, especially his friends. He emerges in these 676 pages as a good-humoured, loveable, amusing fellow who enjoyed his life. In 1997 he wrote to Tony Tanner: 'My own tendency is to be cheerful, to be evasive about ugly things and about my own troubles, to avoid talking about unhappinesses as if to disregard them would be to banish them.'

He continued having fun as he grew older. In 1996, when he was sixty-seven, he wrote to Douglas Chambers: 'We plan on a drug marathon to bring in the New Year. That's what I did last new years, for 3 days... If I get a heart attack, tell them all I died smiling.'

For Jaccottet

KIT HANAFIN

Light and Astonishment

A figure descends from the massif
to stand with its shadow
lengthening at its feet
on the revolving stage of the plain
the matinée is about to finish
the world turns, the prompter turns
a page in his copy of the script
the chestnut trees grow darker,
subtracting other players
from the drama which ends
with a breath slowly exhaled,
at night the same figure
walks in the garden and waits
for the sound of the same breath

*

Darkness is not the opposite
of light, 'joy' is 'too strong'
for the astonishment, no
the *mute* astonishment you feel
as you work your way
through this habitable text, nature
and its restless shadows scrawled
on the valley all of a piece –
later, beneath the bed covers
you read the book of daylight,
as the stars come out to chide you:
sleep now, from its cowl of snow
the sphinx of the mountain
watches over you

*

Morning, and a pale grey wash
lies on the rock above the snowline
the thought of a bus route marked
on a map, or the name of a bird,
would amount to a distraction now,
as one landscape glimpsed
in another, or winter inferred
from autumn, would set you apart
from what is here and what is yours
and yet one scene succeeds
the next like cards dealt face up
on a baize-top table late at night,
you slump in your seat, half awake
but still in the game

*

The eye is a whispering
observatory, o is for sight
mirrored in the verb to look
o is for hearing what the world
we see would have us say of it
without our knowing
what it had in mind
for us to say, or not at first,
o as in poem, reckoning, world
the mistral speaks your words
in its northerly voice,
you look out at the valley
addressed by the valley
and prepare to reply in kind

*

A woodcutter thins down
the burnished juniper,
easy on the shoulder
quickly culled, borne to the stake
to burn like cast antlers –
the flames are barely visible
in sunlight as the tines
crackle, smoke rises,
the huntress has seen him
he may have caught her eye
here is the stag at bay,
dispatch him quickly
with his own axe, do it now
before he bleeds the forest dry

*

In the night the blizzard lets up,
a dusting of snow on the ash trees
is precisely the grandeur
they'd envisaged for the morning,
feigning deference
they bend to the slender mantle
with modest creakings
like romany lyres strung with copper,
tomorrow you'll gaze at the river
where the clouds are doubled
through a band of mist,
thaw is the gate that will open
in front of you, no need to ring
or state your business

Signs

*

At night in the brick hearth
the flames are brighter,
clinging to the logs like ivy

is yours the only shadow here?
in a dream the light of the sky
and the light of the music you heard

were the same light shining
from the lips of the singer

as she paused in the tercet
or sat out the couplets

*

Migration and loss: you ask the swallows
what they mean to carry off
what's the master plan as they head out?

borrow the light of summer on a prayer
bear it away on a wing and return
next year in all good faith

or maybe the'yre scammers, knowing
they've absconded with your life

no dice, they're welcome to your life
but the light is another matter

The vowel sounds are clear
from the shape of her lips, an o
for instance, as if you'd listened

but failed to hear, transfixed
by the visible source of sound –
the consonants are harder to read,

is it 'rebels and all who arm in self-defence'
or 'the sea and the winds grow calm'?
in the heat of the sun,
livestock shelter under the cork oak

*

She sings in the third madrigal
and the manner of her singing
is all that it seemed in the first,

so is the light of her motionless lips,
the light of her eyes, closed
as the parts fall to other singers
and she listens, persuaded:
these are variations on the light

on loan from the sky as you saw it,
the song as you heard it

*

The Convent of La Clarté Notre-Dame

To speak generally of light
or landscape is not to call things
any more or less than themselves,
though names may obscure
what you hoped to address,
the absence of bees
on the gorse for instance,
a dusting of laterite
(maybe Saharan sand) on the oaks,
a bell sounding for vespers
sisters hastening to the cloister,
surprised again by the grace
of heaven & its bright summons
in our lord's allotments

Temples

Sovereign light up on the crags
a handful of medicinal herbs
culled and spread on the table:
arrange them like dusty constellations,
the callused wood is their firmament
you the astronomer, child, healer,
working from memory, late afternoon,
on the disposition of the stars –
vast blue columns of daylight
rise on the footings of the earth,
the dazzling water in a sheep trough
where you plunge your hands
is your premonition of the sky
at night, the table set for supper

*

Palmyra, the temple of Ba'al
the parched race of the Efqa spring,
at dusk the blinding floor of the desert
relents and you walk in the sepia dust
a mile or more from Tadmur prison,
where the enemies of Bashar's father
were murdered, you have lived
a sheltered life you tell yourself
in a severe tone that doesn't suit you –
at home, lifting a towel from the rail
in your bathroom you hear the sound
of someone choking in your basement
you soak the towel in water
press it your face and try to breathe

*

The pillars of a temple and its cornice
are kind of basketwork, the sacred
is richly glimpsed yet withheld from us
by a cage of shadows –
we might live instead beneath the sky
in the enveloping betweenness
of its pale blue columns where nothing
is dissimulated,
    the image of the sun
lodged in its radiant gable lights up
the temple precinct and its parched
hinterland, this is not the light of faith
and power framed in stone,
it keeps no secret under lock and key

*

Wind chill on face and fingers
forces you back to the white ravine
of the bones in contemplation
of the ice core, the marrow of nearly
speechless self whose outer edges
are held in place by gabions,
mesh cells around the detainee –
keys rattle on the lattice,
the year turns and the latch scrapes,
light flattens, the shutters swing
on their hinges and you hear the sound
of the bell at la Clarté Notre-Dame,
the habits of god's willing captives
rustling in his fields of lavender
Boats
Dante, Guido, Lapo, fair sailing,
three poets, three women, six to a skiff,
a wicker hamper, linen napkins –
you try out your bowline knots

on a rope by the landing stage
and assume the third person:
his hands look old, his fingers are weak
the skiffs keep leaving
the mist is building, he's ready to cross
he dreams of a boat with three women,
no poets to speak of, he slips aboard
like a migrant, crouching under a thwart,
an unvoiced syllable,
a breath of wind, a man

*

Miniature vessels full of goods
for the Egyptian dead, provisions
for the other kingdom
whose details glow in the minds
of the devout like exquisite features
of interior design as they thumb
the catalogue and the delicate boats fall
to a child from his box of toys,
he pushes them along the kitchen tiles
in an apartment in Zamalek,
Nasser has hanged his opponents
in the Muslim Brotherhood,
the boats move slowly as the oarsmen
make for the American fridge

*

Bow and stern curve above
the rocking hulls like the horns
of sickle moons, or copper lyres
but the soul has no use for hampers,
maps of the underworld,
beer and charcoal,
crews henceforth will be stood down
at the quays, let the children
with their cedar models play together
at the limits of our world
where the dead hold their peace
a shingle embankment
scored with keel tracks
disappearing at the water's edge

*

Ungaretti gazes at his last flotilla
knowing no living soul
can come alongside, the boats
are foundering, even the waves falter
at this margin of nothingness,
now you must type the word
'seules' for the Italian 'sole',
grains of sand rasp in the carriage
of your olivetti as you draw it
left to right and wait again to hear
the bell ring out for the drowned,
model oars float in the shallows,
and wooden sailors
face down in their white tunics

Balcony

The eye drinks...
'the eye drinks in what is seen'
how else to understand a view,
an arc of hospitality, we're bound
to the giver and the gift,
yet no one owns that seeing,
light falls away, darkness falls
swiftly into place & with all this falling
we could be excused for rising late
on grounds of modesty,
'This is what we've seen,' you say
but 'what have we seen and why?'–
on the balcony you turn
for guidance to your wife

Hands

To welcome a cold spell is to know
it may claim you, the blue tents
of the mountains are vacant now,
pack your version of Homer,
take the gradient, enter at your peril,
rafts in the Aegean founder off the islands,
hands reach out at the point of landfall,
others gesture from the shore,
later they wrap the trembling passengers
like gifts in foil blankets,
even in the shining lake of daylight
dinghies in distress are hard to tell
from breakers in the reach –
at night this ceremony may be fatal

*

A change in the weather carries
damp, invigorating cold down
from the mountains, high
on the shoulders of the rains,
water splashes in the dry courses
Wachet auf, enough is enough
of blinding summer light,
drought in the valleys, autumn
chainsaws wheezing in memoriam,
today the sparkling silvery runs
weave their way into muddy spates,
braiding a rope that will bind
you and deliver you to winter,
here is the rope, here are your hands

'For Jaccottet' is a conversation with two short books by Philippe Jaccottet published in March 2021 by Gallimard within days of his death on 24 February: *La Clarté Notre-Dame* and *Le dernier livre de Madrigaux*. Other works drawn into the exchange include *Leçons* (Payot, 1969), *Beauregard* (Maeght, 1981) and *Pensées sous les nuages* (Gallimard, 1983). The original texts are eloquently present, often in fragmentary versions from all five works. So are several excerpts from Mark Treharne's translations in *Under Clouded Skies* and *Beauregard, Contemporary French Poets: 5* (Bloodaxe, 1994) and Ian Brinton's in *Jaccottet* (Oystercatcher, 2016).

The Fate of Wandering

JENA SCHMITT

Hope Mirrlees, *Paris: A Poem* (Faber) £9.99

If I'd had the chance to visit Paris before the pandemic, I might have walked along Rue de Bouloi, past the green-and-yellow-striped awning of Café de L'Époque, advertisements for Byrrh reflected in the windows, through Galerie Véro-Dodat, one of the nineteenth-century covered passageways Walter Benjamin writes about in *The Arcades Project* (1927–44), with its diamond-shaped marble walkway, Corinthian columns, peaked skylights and filigreed ceiling. I might drop my bag off at a hotel near Palais-Royal, buy a brioche Suisse from a pâtisserie along the way, the Louvre close by now, past Jeanne d'Arc in the Place des Pyramides, through the Portes de Lions entrance towards the Cour Napoléon, where an ornate caryatid supports the upper level of Pavillon Mollien, two more holding hands at the Pavillon de la Bibliothèque, their tunics light, wavering, one slipping from her right breast.

After zigzagging back and forth across the Seine – Jardin des Plantes, Musée d'Orsay, Shakespeare and Company, the charred spires of Notre-Dame – I might hop onto Line 1 of the Métro to Père-Lachaise Cemetery – if there's time – to the graves of Colette, Proust, Oscar Wilde, Modigliani, Chopin, Maria Callas, Molière, the stately cenotaph of Héloïse and Abélard. As Héloïse wrote to Abélard in the 1100s (a book of letters I found at a university library in Toronto in the 1990s): 'Instead of sanctifying myself by a life of penitence, I have confirmed my reprobation. What a fatal wandering!'

Over one hundred years ago the poet Hope Mirrlees (1887–1978) wandered around a seemingly different Paris, just after World War I and the outbreak of Spanish influenza. Only a few years before, sandbags protected monuments; masterpieces relocated from museums for safekeeping; storefront windows taped in geometric patterns to keep glass from shattering; taxis, rather than shuttling customers, drove soldiers to the battlefront; a life-size replica of Paris on the northern outskirts – metro stations, train, illuminated lampposts, a Champs-Élysées – meant to divert night bombings from destroying the city, the war finally ending before it was put to use.

The approximately 450-line *Paris* was published by Virginia Woolf and Leonard Woolf at The Hogarth Press in 1920, the first edition of 175 copies mistaking the year 1919 as its publication date. Although misspellings and other errors slipped past Mirrlees's last-minute corrections and changes, this particular oversight – if it is an oversight – is curious – 1919, 1920. What a difference a year can make. And I say *approximately* 450 lines because some of the poem's lines are so long they run onto the next (sometimes only an *-ly* left dangling). Sometimes, as with 'There is no lily of the valley', the phrase runs

vertically, one letter per line (24 lines, then?). There are two bars of music with the word *Hussh* above them, and so I couldn't decide if that counted as one, two or three. Some of the poetry is not poetry but prose, and should these sections count as lines at all? What of the seven staggered asterisks falling like snow after 'JE VOUS SALUE PARIS PLEIN DE GRACE'? And '3 Rue de Beaune / Paris / Spring 1919' at the end of the poem (printed as *Spring 1916*, the 6 changed to a 9 in pencil supposedly by Woolf herself, at least in the British Library copy online)?

With its varied formatting and typography (justification, alignment, spacing, font size, letter case – a feat of typesetting for Woolf, who had recently acquired a printing press, where letters had to be placed one at a time in a frame or chase to form words – backwards), *Paris* appeared in print two years before T.S. Eliot's *The Waste Land*, after which it flickered in and mostly out of sight for nearly a century. In 2007, writer and critic Julia Briggs (1943–2007) helped to revive interest, deeming it a 'lost masterpiece of modernism' and it was reprinted in *Gender in Modernism: New Geographies, Complex Intersections* (2007). It also appeared in *Collected Poems*, edited by Sandeep Parmar and published by Carcanet Press in 2011, and, most recently, the way it originally appeared, in its entirety, as *Paris: A Poem* (with the added '*A Poem*' in the title just to be clear), by Faber & Faber in 2020, a foreword by Deborah Levy, a commentary by Briggs, an addendum and afterword by Parmar – unfortunately, without the jaunty red, blue and gold harlequin pattern of the original cover.

Paris: A Poem has never been as well-known as Eliot's fervently studied *Waste Land*, to be sure, though the existing scholarly papers are as intriguing as they are plentiful – 'Hope Mirrlees and the Archive of Modernism'; 'The Poet and the Ghosts Are Walking the Streets'; 'A Poetics of Occasion'; 'Disfiguration and Desire: The Erotic Historiography of Hope Mirrlees' *Paris: A Poem*'; 'Modernism's Other Waste Land'; 'Myths of Passage: Paris and Parallax'; 'Poetry as Preservation Ritual: Jane Harrison, Antiquarianism and Hope Mirrlees's *Paris*': 'Recrossing the Ritual Bridge: Jane Ellen Harrison's Theory of Art in the Work of Hope Mirrlees'; 'Modernism's Lost Hope: Virginia Woolf, Hope Mirrlees and the Printing of *Paris*', 'Whatever Happens, Some Day It Will Look Beautiful' – all of which have revealed valuable connections and vantages of *Paris* in the last few decades.

Dense with references, the poem does require studious determination and quite a bit of unpacking. Not to mention it makes Apollinaire's calligram, 'La Tour Eiffel' (1913), look like child's play. Take this snippet, for instance:

Some Pasteur made the Gauls immune
Against the bite of Nymphs... look

Gambetta
A red stud in the button-hole of his frock-coat
The obscene conjugal *tutoiment*
Mais c'est logique.

The Esprit Français is leaning over him,
Whispering

Secrets
exquisite   significant
fade   plastic

Thank goodness for Google, I kept thinking, or else I might not know what Mirrlees was talking about. If I were living in 1920, would I be able to go to a library and find everything I needed to – 'Madame Récamiers', 'Grand Seigneur from Brittany', 'Yearning for "Work and Days"', 'The lovely Spirit of the Year', '*Pigeon vole*', 'Grand Guignol of Catholicism', 'Bossuet', and so on? What if I had children to take care of – 'the *eidola* in hideous frames' – laundry piling up – 'MORT AU CHAMP D'HON-NEUR' – floors to clean – '*Poilus* in wedgewood blue' – everyone always hungry – 'Triptolemos in swaddling clothes'? What if I didn't have the luxury of sitting with Virginia Woolf in her garden discussing art, the chance for Woolf to look at me, the way she looked at Mirrlees, then write to her friend Margaret Llewelyn Davies:

Dearest Margaret,

... Last weekend... we had a young lady who changed her dress every night for dinner – which Leonard and I cooked, the servants being on holiday. Her stockings matched a wreath in her hair: every night they were differently coloured; powder fell about in flakes, and the scent was such we had to sit in the garden. Moreover, she knows Greek and Russian better than I do French; is Jane Harrison's favourite pupil, and has written a very obscure, indecent and brilliant poem, which we are going to print. It's a shame that all this should be possible to the younger generation; still I feel that *something* must be lacking, don't you? We had Maynard Keynes to entertain her, since we could offer little in the way of comfort...

What if I didn't have servants who couldn't cook because they were on holiday? Too tired to go to the library, the library closed, no libraries nearby? Couldn't afford childcare, books, didn't have access to an internet connection, let alone matching stockings and wreaths, which I thought were for doors, not the top of one's head? If I don't know Mirrlees's references offhand – 1919, 1920, 2019, 2020, 2021 even – what does that mean for the poem itself? If *Paris* feels impermeable, as it sometimes does, what is its true effect? And why am I being hard on a poem I am so fond of?

For *Paris: A Poem* is as sturdy as a monument, a meticulous building upon of English and French phrases, ekphrastic moments, fragments of observations, sensations, slogans, advertisements, conversations, literature, works of art, gaps and holes left over from bombs and gunfire, antisemitism, immigration, workers' strikes, religion, sexism, gender inequality, a battle for and against the bourgeoisie, of which Mirrlees was a part, her family's wealth the reason she could live the life she did, travelling here and there, a former teacher, Jane Harrison, thirty-seven years her senior – mentor? lover? friend? confidante? everyone always wants to know – by her side until Harrison died, wherein Mirrlees retreated to South Africa for decades, whittling away the blasphemous allusions in *Paris* ('le petit Jésus fait pipi', perhaps, or President Wilson happily smelling 'the diluvial / urine of Gargantua') and writing an obscure two-book biography about Sir Robert Bruce Cotton. ('If poets could only be antiquaries!' she exclaims in *A Fly in Amber: Being an Extravagant Biography of the Romantic Antiquary Sir Robert Bruce Cotton*. 'For antiquaries alone among mortals can restore the past, and preserve the present, tangibly – and it is touch that matters most'.)

'I want a holophrase', Mirrlees imparts – perhaps demands – in the very first line of *Paris*, a term first coined by Harrison as 'a statement of relations', where meaning is compressed into a single compact referential word, a self-sustaining signifier that has the ability to expand open given the chance, one that encompasses time and experience into a specific amaranthine moment, instantaneously crystallized, a boundless, redoubtable here-there. *Paris* is filled with holophrases, then, beginning with the title, stacked one on top of the other to create an almost living, breathing artifact the reader might look up to, walk around, pass through, the poem suddenly three-dimensional, one grand, statuesque holophrase. (I cannot help but think *Paris* best read, not left to right, from page to page, but vertically, one long curvesome read.) 'The Scarlet Woman shouting BYRHH and deafening / St. John at Patmos' – imagine how loud she would have to be, how emphatic, how necessary. Perhaps stronger, more persuasive, imperative, when they gather – the Fates, the sibyls, the Sirens: 'The Sirens stand, as it would seem, to the ancient and the / modern', writes Harrison, in the epilogue of Mirrlees's fantasy novel, *Lud-in-the-Mist*, published in 1926. '[F]or the impulses in life as yet immortalised, imperious longings, ecstasies, whether of love or art...'.

This duality – ancient, modern, longing, ecstasy, love, art – helixes around *Paris*, constricting and restraining the poem long after it is read. There is passivity and opposition, assurance and uncertainty, aimlessness and focus, comedy and seriousness, pessimism and hope, wealth and poverty, disbelief and faith, hardness and sentimentality – a multitude of observances and attitudes, tones and opinions that lack attributes and defining features, and so can be as confounding as they are bombardingly discordant. In some instances, lines that may not have been given second thought in 1920 sound even harsher in the present:

THE CHILDREN EAT THE JEW

PHOTO MIDGET

Lizard-eyes
Assyrian beards...

The tart little race, whose brain, the Arabs said, was one of the three perches of the Spirit of God.

Crotchets and quavers have the heads of niggers and they writhe in obscene syncopation.

The bulbs were votive offerings
  From a converted Jap

The whores like lions are seeking their meat from God.
  (from *Paris*, The Hogarth Press, 1919)

These expose, intentionally or unintentionally, the tatters and terribleness of an age, bringing into question the attitudes and opinions that ultimately inform Mirrlees's vision, and how much it can be admired. Whose voice is Mirrlees's voice, after all? But there is also something whirring – unspoken, resistant, subversive, indefatigable – just beneath the surface, ready to take hold. '*I don't like the gurls of the night-club – they love women*', an unnamed someone quips, the next line following: '*Toutes les cartes marchent avec une allumette!*' ('All cards work with a match!')

I started to look at *Paris: A Poem* the way I first began to think about Paris itself, all sights and sounds and smells, strength and conviction and feeling, of being able to walk around a version of the city, to be a visitor, a voyeur, the way Mirrlees once was, descending into the depths of the underground, hearing *messieursetdames*, no space between them, male and female neologistically one. As though one might walk freely in the middle of the night, without worry, the *brekekekek koax koax* (or *coax coax*, as Mirrlees writes) of Aristophanes's frogs taunting Dionysus under the Seine, lights sparkling along the darkening dark, four brass allegories along the Pont Mirabeau – Abundance, Paris, Commerce, Navigation – leading the way, a place, if momentary, to be a part of.

Within the mythological topography of Paris, muses Benjamin in *The Arcades Project*, past the threshold of its gates and triumphal arches, one transforms. Only a ghost could cover so much ground in a day, and what vertiginous roaming – the Arc de Triomphe 'Square and shadowy like Julius Caesar's dreams', the Tuileries 'in a trance', 'The background gray and olive-green' of the Louvre, 'Hidden courts / With fauns in very low-relief piping among lotuses', carpets of crocuses and Chionodoxa, paintings and sculptures out in the open ('Pietà of Avignon, / L'Olympe, / Giles, / Mantegna's Seven Deadly Sins, / The Chardins'), Anna Karenina coming and going, Molière, Voltaire, Freud, Madame Victor-Hugo, someone shouting 'Taxis, / Taxis, / Taxis', the sky 'saffron behind the two towers of Nôtre- / Dame'. 'Scorn the laws of geometry', Mirrlees continues elsewhere, 'Step boldly into the wall of the Salle Caillebotte', along with many more streets, gardens, galleries, shops. 'In the Ile Saint-Louis [sic], in the rue Saint Antoine, in / the Place des Vosges / The Seventeenth Century lies exquisitely dying...'.

'*....le paysage fantomatique des plaisirs et des professions maudites, incompréhensibles hier et que demain ne connaître jamais*', writes Louis Aragon in *Le Paysan de Paris*, quoted by Benjamin as '[p]laces that yesterday were incomprehensible, and that tomorrow will never know', and echoed in Victor Hugo's *La Fin de Satan*:

As for your cities, Babels of monuments
Where all events clamour at once,
How substantial are they? Arches, towers, pyramids –
I would not be surprised if, in its humid incandescence,
The dawn one morning suddenly dissolved them...

For Mirrlees, moments and monuments are indeed substantial. Though some may suddenly dissolve or disappear, they are revisited, memorialized, in *Paris*, and in her formal later poems, such as partway through 'The Rendez-Vous', where an 'I' admits, 'For me it was in Paris thirty-odd years ago / At the collected paintings of Berthe Morisot', and a 'weary, exiled Charles Baudelaire' wanders the streets in 'Et in Arcadia Ego':

An uninvited spectre seems to loom,
That of an old and half-forgotten friend,
Whose lonely grave in Montparnasse,
Forsaken save by weeds and grass,
Long ago I used to tend.

After reading 'I was dead too not very long ago' in Mirrlees's poem 'Sickness and Recovery at the Cape of Good Hope in Spring', a poem about being turned away from Hades, 'too old to be Persephone', I look back to Harrison, who, in *Aspects, Aorists and the Classical Tripos* (1919), writes: 'The step out of the actual into the remembered and the hoped for is really a leap of tremendous genius'. And in another place:

Abstraction then rather than *achievement* is – if I am right – from the outset the very pith and marrow of the perfective... The perfective is the aorist, not indefinite, ill-defined in time, but *out of time*, remote from *durée*, as [Henri] Bergson would say, free from the hot intimacy of personal experience.

Wandering away again – where are the Fates when I need them – Mirrlees might find herself, or maybe this time it is me, walking 'through the burning cathedral of the summer' that Violette Leduc writes about in *Folie en Tête*, or *Mad in Pursuit* (1971), along the banks of Canal Saint-Martin, the bougainvillea in full fiery bloom against the water's eerie blue-green. Somewhere along Rue Bichat – or is it Rue Alibert – doors open to another courtyard garden; a window displays *pastel de nata*, *bola de Berlim*, *trança*, *queijadas*, *croissants aux amandes*; a drawing of a woman on the wall of an empty storefront holds flowers and foliage in front of her face, her unadorned body all nerve-endings. Later, at the highest point of Parc des Buttes-Chaumont, once a garbage dump, an abattoir, a quarry, now looking out from the Temple de la Sybille fifty metres up, it is clear: there is still so much to see. What would Mirrlees think, in nearby Le Marais, of the bullet holes left in the sunlit mosaic of Jo Goldenberg's delicatessen; the Moroccan-owned épicerie, Au Marché du Marais, replaced by a Princesse Tam Tam lingerie chain; the pop-up stores that appear as quickly as they disappear; the rows of brightly coloured €5, €7 and €10 bouquets at HAPPY fleuriste? Back at Les Halles, where *Paris* begins and ends, the vast underground shopping at Forum des Halles; the kitchenware store, E. Dehillerin, spanning the corner of 18-20 Rue Coquillière since 1890; the delicious handmade *lamien* at Les Pâtes Vivantes?

Whether thirty years ago, one hundred, one hundred and one or two, Mirrlees's *Paris* has always been a holophrase. Impatient and restless, energetic and demanding, it is filled with a maelstrom of memories and perceptions, a reconstruction, however imperfect, however imposing and hermetic, after the ravages of war, after the ravages of age and expectation and recollection, of a city that no longer exists, one that never existed. And yet, as Mirrlees, writes in 'The Rendez-Vous': 'So either in the chiaroscuro of To-day, / Or stylized in mosaics of Ravenna / The scene can be depicted and be true'.

Five Poems

MARIANNA GEIDE

Translated from the German by James Womack

august rhapsody

1.
i falling fell
against heaven's fabric, instinct with desire,
against the compacted air, damp earth, thick roots,
the layered turf, the earth's white matter,
her fire-hot seeds
that poured their heat to the earth
and the earth was made desert, unseen,
        judged innocent,
and she refused food, refused
        to name names,
began to turn round another's axis.
now they call her Moon.

2.
the mirror reflects the face that butts it;
kicks off the fight and wins it easily,
but the blow's force makes the face shatter:
once one, now five look back at me.

can parts be greater than the whole they're made of?
in all five pieces i'm the same me.
can my face be carried off,
forever hidden away?

i falling fell,
broke it into five bits.
ins Kristall, he says, *bald dein Fall, ins Kristall,*
und was wirst du machen in diesem Falle,
try to cancel it all out.

3.
then they put the earth to death.
how'd they do that stuff?
first jabbed with a knife, then
an invisible sickle, then
slit its gut with a static mouth,
a black-pink mouth.

they begged in vain:
the grains of corn
in the mouth of iron

buckwheat flakes
in their firm armour,
their darts and spears

spikes of oats

tried in vain to pierce the sky.
earth was not the sky's to kill,
but the sky saw it all.

4.
with a crash the lightning caught up with him
with a crash the lightning caught him up
gluier, sticking the pages together
no one cared about reading any longer
the Lamb lifts up the broken face,
the Lamb does not touch
the first seal, the second seal,
he is sad, filled with bygone years and undone scars.
phosphorus in his footsteps, neon in his palms,

radium in his blood,
uranium his heart.

5.
pistachio shells, mussel casings,
flowers like no one ever saw –
rotten apples, ripe eggplants,
heading off to distant lands,
clinging to the keel,
they sang, they sang so.

they clung to one another and sang:
whenever we possibly can
we cover your body close
and let our petals close
and keep you from harm.

now we swim freely
and leave you by the sea.

psalm 1

unknown noises punched me in the belly,
unknown noises wanted me to die,
flapped their wings against my head,
transformed themselves to water and to bread,
assaulted me like I was their slave, or
      like I was their saviour,
assaulted me like I was dead,
      and then resurrected
        and just walked off,
to recall forever in my throat and mouth
        this white noise
    for which the world has no use.

psalm 2

the angel with the face of the sun peers into my pad
from the lamp under its little shade,
the angel with the face of the sun is here for my mind,
here to take it and set it alight.
'when I paused in my work, where were you?'
he asks, 'where were you
when round my table there sat
the ones with whose mouths I now eat?
where were you at the end of creation;
and whose fingers meshed
in my sunday flesh,
and now dabble in your skin?'
the angel with the face of the sun peeks
into my head
and I am struck dumb.
the angel with the face of the sun takes
me, for good,
to his home.

psalm 3

(*the cradle will rock*)

they spilled me into a carousel, made me feel ill,
i was reeled and lulled,
they did not swaddle me, swill me, let me fall,
did not unfurl me then lull me,
they killed me and lulled me,
i must have been their beloved idol.
they didn't bury me with a shovel,
set above me a title,
they laid others on me, and me on them.
and never gave me a name.

psalm 4

(*we will cradle you*)

the golden sand runs through the fingers of distant hands,
the golden sand,
they washed it in water, brushed it off heads, let it climb legs,
pulled it from crimson caves,
took some from the depths of eyes,
for this was war
and they thought it was nobody's.
and there were so few things left on the earth.

Now... the trees

BRIAN MORTON

Now, mostly, I tend the trees. They fill a long lozenge of land, on the opposite side of the burn from the house. When we came, it was a dense thicket of dying spruce, punctuated dramatically by three large poplars. It was planted to spite a previous owner who wanted to buy back the land to build on, and was placed on the replanting plan, which requires a proportion of clear-felled hill to be restored to broadleaf. We went to the landowner, to ask if we could claim back our *irredenta,* a marshy field to the north of house and the little wood. He and his land agent sucked their teeth for a while and went away. Two days later a letter arrived agreeing that the land was ours as long as we remained here, but with two conditions: no building and that we take responsibility for replanting and protection of the new trees.

The old wood had seemed huge and dark and biologically dead at the centre. The only sign of life was the keyring jingle of crossbills looking for seeds in the upper storey; that, and an occasional owl pellet. As the trees came down, to be turned into firewood, we replaced them with the natives specified on the plan: oak and alder, rowan, crab apple and goat willow. I sneaked in a few beeches and tolerated an opportunistic cotoneaster *sinensis*, a seed dropped by a passing bird. The decision was vindicated when I went out one winter morning to find the tree covered in garrulous waxwings, small, parroty birds that irrupt during cold Scandinavian winters, looking for berries. These are the birds of John Shade's poem in Nabokov's *Pale Fire* where the waxwing is "slain / by the false azure of the window pane". We hang a fiberglass peregrine in front of the house's only large window, to prevent any such unpoetic fate befalling our brightest visitors.

*

The trees are mostly planted in clusters, almost all of them dedicated to absent family, friends and friends of friends. My mother's ashes are there, under an oak. The only solitaries are the crab apples, Daniel Boones of the sylvan world, who demand space away from their own kind. Some have accused us of something similar.

*

In Scotland, a house move is called a 'flit' and that is how our coming felt; hasty, almost furtive, the way refugees must move. We had a deadline. The shooting estate where we had rented for nearly ten years was going on the market, broken up by divorce and ostentatiously bad business. We tried to buy the house and field, but our florid landlord, Napoleonic to the last, insisted he would only sell with a second house and a hundred acres of scrubby glen to which he would still retain the shooting rights. Hasty leaving somewhat blunted the

pain of going. The urgent search for somewhere new delayed homesickness for a time.

In the event, we were sent the wrong house details but our eye was caught by mention of an oratory where normally you would expect en-suite bedrooms, modernised kitchens and double garages. We visited, on a day when the grass was dancing with orange-tip butterflies and fell in love on the rebound. We went home, sold some old books and pictures, borrowed some money from our mothers, and made the monks what to anyone else would have been an insultingly low offer. They had moved on by that stage, and were happy to accept. We moved in on a midge-ridden July night with no breeze. It was a warning that evening strolls in summer were unlikely to feature.

The house has a number of eccentricities. The oratory is a converted byre, with panelled walls and a raised platform for the altar and sanctuary. It's a prayerful space, lit only by two dim skylights. The crucifix is mad of reclaimed timber, the corpus shaped out of fence wire. There's a Sacred Heart, too, very different from the usual cardiology-textbook illustrations. The local priest isn't keen to celebrate Mass there. The monks who preceded us are excommunicates now but their shadow extends backward.

*

Their place has been taken by blackbirds. It took time to realise that not only do they sing at night, but they actually seem to keep the hours of the Holy Office, singing at intervals, spending the rest of their time studiously avoiding one another, picking quietly through the leaf-litter. The song seems to change, as if there were a different melody for Matins and Terce, Vespers and Lauds. It's the males who gather here. The brown-habited females seem to keep away, in the sister-houses that ring the wood.

*

The trees provide the most peaceful work we have. When felled, the wood was left dotted with treacherous stumps and ankle-twisting roots. Removing stumps by hand is killing work, but we happened across a method that quietly, slowly clears the ground, and affords a litt Once the noisy part is over, that is. With the chainsaw we make a couple of deep cuts through the stump, more if it is large; smaller ones look like a capital *theta,* larger ones a compass rose. Then we light a little fire with straw and twigs – larger pieces of wood only scorch and don't work. As the fire is steadily fed, always with tiny sticks, the glowing embers fall down into the sawcuts and smoulder there. On a breezy day, clogging ash is blown away. On still days, we crouch and blow through little lengths of pipe until we are dizzy. After a while, the wood itself becomes its own fuel. We climb up to the house at dusk and look back at clusters of soft red glow, Israelite tents on a far plain.

In the morning, if they are not still burning, all that's left are a few blackened cusps, like a tramp's teeth. They're charcoal brittle and easily kicked off. Sometimes a second fire is needed to get rid of stubborn remnants. It was while sitting by a quietly ticking stump, hypnotised by the pulsing glow of embers in a late afternoon wind, that I first caught sight of Teuchter.

*

She – it never occurred to me that she was anything but she – came out of the bracken a hundred feet away, just a head and then shoulders and then the long, low body and massive tail. She was intensely alert, knowing I was there, but somewhat mollified by my immobility and maybe reassured by the mixed scents, smoke and human, that must have been circulating. She stood for a very long time, looking as it were past me, while I affected to look at some point above her. We stayed like that for some time. In the end, I didn't see her go. One second, she was there; the next, the bracken had swallowed her.

Wild cats in Scotland were never common, in human times at least, but as populations have shrunk and breeding distances grown larger, individuals have been forced ever closer to human habitation and thus ever closer to domestic cats. Where once they remained distinct, they now certainly interbreed, yielding feral populations of strikingly mixed appearance. Teuchter had all the marks of a classic wildcat, flattened head with small, tucked ears, short legs relative to the body, and the giveaway tail, but, more than that, some essence of, there's no other word, pure wildness came off her. I'm not a wishful wildlife watcher. My first instinct, on seeing a possible rarity, is denial. Last summer, I shook my head dolefully as we watched a harrier quarter the field in late afternoon light. It seemed to have some of the marks of a Montagu's – rare here, rare enough anywhere to have once been a whole *Archers* storyline – rather than the somewhat more common hen harrier that still has a stronghold around us, where there are few persecuting gamekeepers. I watched for half an hour, unconvinced that the rusty splotches on the underwings were anything more than an artefact of light, muttering 'Nah... nope... can't be' and leaving the bird unticked on the home list. A week later, a Montagu's was spotted and photographed a mile down the road. Still, it's a less disillusioning cast of mind than assuming that every brown blob in a hedge is a Siberian rarity.

With Teuchter, I kept an open mind. The name is a kind of cultural slur, meaning 'northern, untamed, illiterate', less commonly used now than its opposite, that music-hall favourite 'Sassenach'. But it seemed to fit. I read around the subject and found myself deep in the complexities of introgressive hybridization, dominant and subordinate gene pools. Instinct suggested she might be wild. I'd grown up elsewhere in the county, where wild cats were known to breed on the high boggy tops that never seemed to attract walkers or campers. Once you've seen one, there is probably no mistaking.

A fortnight later, she crossed the road in front of my wife's car. I'm not a wishful watcher, but also not a solitary one. Like the hole in one at golf when no one in watching, an unconfirmed and unphotographed sighting of anything is always subject to doubt, even self-doubt. She crossed the road low and fast and melted into the verge. I leapt out and caught her on the far side, just as she was about to disappear among the stunted alders. She turned for a moment, glared and then again dematerialised.

*

The following spring I was checking tree guards and posts on the far side of the plantation where a brown tsunami of bracken yearly threatens to swamp the area but yet manages to stay unbroken at a certain distance, frozen like a Hokusai print. I was crouching, absorbed, when I became aware of tiny sounds, a short but somehow sharp mewling from deep in the bracken. It was unmistakably the cry of hungry kittens. I stood irresolute for a while, certain I could find the spot, but unwilling to wade in, not so much afraid of an encounter with a hissing mother as unable to take the disappointment of little black or ginger or tortoiseshell faces. Days later, the postman reported a biggish cat carrying something in its mouth at the hairpin turn, but he's as vague on zoological detail as he is on addresses. We routinely pass on bills and birthday cards to neighbours down the glen, while they sheepishly hand us back long-dated missives from HMRC and DWP which we've stoutly – and truly – denied ever receiving. None of the local farmers has reported a wildcat, though old John remembers them from past years. We've never seen Teuchter again.

*

I made a vow when we moved here. Not that I would never move again. I had tried that once and watched it crumble. This time, I promised I would sow or plant something every day of the year. It's a tiny gesture of faith, but easy enough to keep up. The winter months are taken up with tree planting, or rather, pushing bare-root twigs – oak, goat willow, crab apple, alder – into muddy slits cut with a spade. I work at them like a boxer's cornerman, dabbing away the red ooze, pinching the earth closed and tight, rubbing Vaseline onto the stem to deter nibbling voles, finishing with a sprinkle of wood ash. Some fail to take or are trampled by deer. Some dislike the wet and grow at a creeping pace. Others inexplicably rise above their environment and put on brave growth in spring, before ducking down again to gather strength through another winter.

A sapling oak snapped at head height, weakened by a too-vigorous burst of growth. I planned to grub it up and replace it but never got round to it and the following spring it threw out exuberant arms and now grows on, still short and stubby but with branches that will thicken and sag over time. The stub of its original trunk is a favourite early evening spot for the tawny owl, who sits there peacefully, a still extension of the wood but for the fierce eyes. The ground around is littered with his pellets, turd-shaped, musty cylinders of compressed hair that we pull apart to reveal entire vole skulls, impressing and appalling visiting children. The owl has a disconcerting habit of flying low and silently overhead. It feels like your own personal Fuseli nightmare.

*

Winter is also the time we plant our garlic. It's our only real cash crop, grown in large amounts and sold furtively at hotel kitchen doors for cash in hand. It thrives on a cold winter and then gallons of water at the height of the growing season. For a time we had what I believed was our very own strain, a pinkish sport I found in the middle of a row. When the flower head emerged I shaved off the outer parts to prevent pollination and saved the tiny bulbils that remained. They grew on slowly and it was three years before we took a crop from them, but they retained the pinkish skin and sweet, heady smell. They thrived for two seasons, then in the third all died at once, yellowing in the ground and leaving a sulphurous stink. At school, I could never tell a carpel from a pistil, but now I spend unhealthy hours quietly pulling apart the flowering parts of our cropping plants, exploring the mysteries of the *gynoecium* – how wonderful that it's called the 'woman's house', *gynaikos oikia* – examining the tiny pollinators, little wasps only millimetres long, that seem to have taken the place of bumblebees and honeybees. Of those, we see distressingly few now. I long to keep bees again, but fear that something in the land here discourages and weakens them. Last summer, a swarm settled under the soffits of the hen house, a treacly, rippling mass edged with an iridescent corona of shifting wings, but it was gone before the local beekeeper could drive down and secure them. They were dark bees and I had hopes they were a wild species from the islands. The only other time we had a population was when they colonised a crack in the oratory wall and settled somewhere between the stonework and the panelling. We could put our ears to the wood inside, just below the sanctuary step and feel rather than hear the industrious hum within. Morning prayer on a still morning seemed to be accompanied by a soft drone note, but it may have been imaginary. So, too, a faint stain on the panelling, which we convinced ourselves carried a whiff of honey.

*

It wouldn't be a paradise if there weren't snakes. The glen is famous for adders. Everyone has a story of collie dogs coming home, chapfallen and sickly from a bite. We still wonder if the children's ginger cat, found dead one morning just above the house, had been 'stung', as they still like to say here. We more often see them dead on the road, lying like broken fan-belts, but in summer it's wiser not to put a hand down on rocks as you lever your way up the hill. They bask on warm rocks, little coils of black chevrons. Mostly, though, they're shy, and all you might hear is the quick susurrus of the skin against dry stalks. Grass snakes, which move differently, are said to make a different sound, but it's only distinguishable by the kind of people who can turn round during the Adagietto and whisper that the second viola is a quarter tone sharp.

Ticks are more of a worry, but we don't walk about in the long grass and bracken in sandals or shorts. One already hot morning, still quite early in spring, I went out to find a big snake coiled on the doorstep and I've found them sunning on unburnt stumps in the wood. The Englishwoman who lives further down the glen was trapped in her kitchen by one that took her Welcome mat to heart and settled there for the afternoon. Far more common, though, are slow worms, smooth aluminium shapes that seem to extrude out of tussocks and weave a molten path through the grass. Occasionally the hens find one and fall on it ritually, plumed Incas at a sacrifice, screaming in joy as each takes turns to peck the writhing lizard, for that's what they really are. Common lizards are plentiful, too, especially round the stone fanks that have been turned into growing beds and cold frames. They're confiding, materialising right next to a planting hand, breathing and winking before slipping away in search of flies.

***

We find we're either looking down or looking up, which might explain the incidence of bruising. When I took my son to the GP to investigate possible asthma, she took in the purple-and-yellow marks across his back and ribcage with a more than usually pursed mouth. We waited for Social Services to call, hoping that 'falls down while looking for the eagle' would be sufficient explanation. Visitors rush in excitedly to say that there's an eagle in the garden, which means invariably that it's a buzzard. They nest nearby and the youngsters circle around on early summer mornings, crying plaintively, worrying the hens but too feckless to launch a serious attack. To see the eagle, which comes over from an eyrie on the Atlantic cliffs, you need to focus much higher and be lucky enough to pick out the majestic signature and slow, circling flight. In warm weather, a single wingbeat, or often just a relaxed glide will take her from one side of the glen to the other. Looking up sometimes brings other bonuses, other than sore ribs. Twice, I've seen a more angular bird, slighter in aspect but with a faintly military air: a migrating osprey, heading north. There's a lochan in the hills, edged with old Scots pines and we've looked there in hope that a pair might settle and nest, but there isn't enough either water or fish to sustain a brood.

Then one morning, something exceptional: an eagle, obviously, but more massive by a considerable factor. It looked like a flying door. White-tailed sea eagles have been released at locations down the West coast and are now breeding again. First-generation birds are tagged, but it was impossible to see and its passage was over in seconds. 'Ernes', as they're still sometimes beautifully known, sometimes drift inland, just because they can. The Gaelic for golden eagle is 'iolaire', which is more lyrically beautiful, as the bird itself deserves. Climb enough to get near the cliff edges and there is sometimes a glimpse of one gliding at eye-level or, even more stirringly, below, its tawny hood and ruff caught in the sunlight. Those moments go in deep and stir something ancient.

In dreams, which come in unvarying clusters, often at the turning of the seasons, I see the house and wood as from a great height: the trees grown into a thick canopy that hides the blackened stumps, the roof fallen in, shrubs and fireweed growing where the rooms were, the outline of the lazy-beds still visible in the field. We're not there; only the trees...

Parmenides on the Boardwalk

JEFFREY WAINWRIGHT

Out on the boardwalk today for another 'health walk'.
It keeps our feet out of the watery ground.
As usual I stop by the tree-stump decorated
with a fungus nicely confined between
splits in the wood and the curve of the bark.
Another dog passes by, as eager as ever.
Today the fungus is the pale green of a paint-chart
and is hard to the touch, plaster-like, resistant.
Is it dried and dead or in yet another phase?
If dead what was the life that has been lost?

No matter there is life everywhere,
energy in every form.
Velvet mosses clothe the bark of fallen trees;
turn up a log and shiny grubs protest at the light;
in the turbid pools the hog-louse nudges past
the ravenous nymphs of the damsel fly –
the beautiful demoiselle; leaves gleam freshly
in the reviving undergrowth; garlic
awaits its flowers; blackthorn vaunts its snowy clouds;
bacteria will be hereabouts striving furiously
as they do in yoghourt and in sourdough,
simple souls but hard as nails, their plasmids
and their daughter cells, their flagellas,
some of them, beating always towards the light.
All this comes by book or the information board
we also use to spot a bulky thrush, a robin
or that pert and fussy wren – are their 'songs'
as material as a ribosome?   Another question.

Look, is that Parmenides, sandalled as we might
    expect,
avoiding a springer on a too-long lead?
He's valuing sense enough here,
a trip or fall would interrupt philosophy.
Further down the boardwalk that must be his goddess
waiting to accost him once again.   Her cagoule is

perfect.
I edge closer to listen in to what she says.
She seems to think Parmenides needs a refresher
on the One since Plato dragged it to his cave
and made of it a fashionable Idea or Form
not something solid like the ribosome.
Others, she warns, are so in thrall to the jazzy tumult
of the world they think that Reason is capsized
and Truth a mirage or a fantasy.

Phew Parmenides, you're going to have a job
getting that into your old hexameters nowadays.
Is what she's saying that the hog-louse, damsel
and bacterium are not a numbered aggregate
of different things but share something
that makes them shift and scurry, predators
and prey, and that makes them One, and us One
with them as we seize our breakfast for another day?

Parmenides shivers in the vexing English breeze
and comes back along the boardwalk.
He nods and that gives me the nerve to speak to him.
This One, I say, is an idea I like
though I'm not sure why – it might be Truth.
I know it's simpler to see gnats swarming
to no tune at all, or starlings as merely particular
and not try to seek the rhyme or reason
of their gatherings.   I hope you are going to set me right.
He puffs his cheeks and makes as though to speak
but then steps off the boardwalk, taking care
where he puts his foot, and disappears.
I walk on, sidling past a mastiff across the path
alert and listening for its owner's call.
The trees resume their patient climb,
the small dishes of fungus ... no - too much to itemise.
The thought-filled sky absorbs it all.
I'm looking for an ending where the cadence falls.

Three Poems after Sophia Parnok

translated from the Russian by

ANNA IVASKEVICA AND ALEX WONG

with the good counsels of Alex Chernova

Evenings slither down, as
            fogs of a pale blue –
Slide from the peaks
      down over the lakes.

Tomorrow, tomorrow and yesterday,
      slip out of mind.

Days are like dreams, they are like
Dreams; and thoughts
Are more submissive to the unaccountable.

I'm alone: but only one who is alone
Is coupled
            with the universe of God.
Inside myself I attend to the secret life
      spilled over in everything. Isn't my heart
Bound with the roots
Of all the flowers
            blooming? And don't our hearts
Beat as in agreement with the whole?

And really, is it not
            mere dream – this struggle of wills?
We are all of us crowned
                  with a single plighting wreath:
That alpine ocean spreads over everything living.

*

It's true, I'm left alone. True, when you left
You sentenced me to an orphanhood of soul.
Alone as the first and only of our kind
      On the first day of its making.

But the prophecy vented then by your vain rage
Is hardly a curse particular to me:
The pure in soul – don't even they, confiding,
      Sing to us about orphanhood?

And they want the best in us, and they're not to be envied,
Who will never – not even once, when filled with grief –
Shudder at that line in Tyutchev: 'How
      Shall anyone else understand you?'

*

To our sinners' paradise: give me a hand and come.
In disregard of heaven's plans and measures,
May returns for us in the middle of winter
And flowers set wild colour in the green.

The apple tree leaned over us there, with fanning
Blossom bent in scented sprays. The earth
Smelled charmingly, like you; there were butterflies
Falling in love, colliding in mid-air.

We're another year older now. Well, what of that?
An old wine, give it one more year laid down,
Grows even smoother with what it knows of ripeness.
My love, my greying Eve, I welcome you.

*

Sophia Parnok, born in 1885, was a Russian poet, translator and librettist. She was also a literary critic of some prescience, who early identified the 'Big Four', as they are still known, of Silver Age Russian poetry: Akhmatova, Tsvetaeva, Pasternak and Mandelstam. Of Jewish descent and later a convert to the Russian Orthodox Church, she was briefly married to the dramatist Vladimir Volkenstein, but her intimate relationships were mostly with women, and her passionate sapphic eroticism is explored with great frankness in her verse. Her lovers included Marina Tsvetaeva, with whom she had a tumultuous affair in 1914–16, and who addressed Parnok in her famous and beautiful sequence, 'Podruga' (which Elaine Feinstein translates under the title 'Girlfriend'). She suffered from Graves' Disease throughout her life, and died in 1933 at the age of forty-eight.

Though she is the subject of one English-language biography, and despite her vivid evocation in some of Tsvetaeva's best-loved lyrics, Parnok's own poems have been little translated into English. The following three pieces (chosen by Anna) are the first fruits of what we hope will be a happy collaboration between one Anna and two Alexes.

Means and Ends

ALICE HILLER AND SASHA DUGDALE

in conversation

Sasha Dugdale: You've told me that you came fairly late to the writing of poetry, and I wanted to begin by asking you about your journey to your first collection *bird of winter*, which is published this year by Pavilion Press. I often think of Penelope Fitzgerald who, when she was asked why she had taken so long to write her novels, is said to have answered, 'I've been busy'. I think you've been very busy with your work, your life and family, but I wonder also if we come to poetry when we are ready to, or when it is ready for us. It isn't something that can be hurried. The genre (in its elusiveness and instability) waits for us to find it.

Alice Hiller: Thank you for that question Sasha. I'm 56, so I agree with Penelope Fitzgerald about having 'been busy' (studying, earning, parenting, bereavement, single parenthood). There was an additional inhibitor for me, of feeling that the waters of my self had been polluted when I was groomed and then sexually abused as a child. Although I always worked with words, for many years, I couldn't articulate my own experience. I wasn't even sure I had a space to speak from – as an artist. Having been a freelance journalist, and then done a Lit Crit PhD, amongst other things, I started trying to write creatively in my forties. My younger son had left for university. It was safer to engage with dangerous energies – because there was no one at home to be hurt if I came apart. I tried a novel. The voice only worked when it broke down into a looser form. I followed this, hesitantly, into Pascale Petit's final course at the Tate. The poems I made arose from silence, and inarticulacy, and enacted themselves through play and experiment, sound work and graphic elements. Mixing darkness and light, child and adult, thought and feeling, offered a way forwards.

Unlike my late-coming self, Sasha, you have a long-standing commitment to this medium, as a poet, editor and translator. *Deformations* is your fifth collection. Can I ask what first made poetry seem both necessary, and possible to you, and how this engagement sits within your larger life? When I was reading the 'Pitysad' section of *Deformations,* emerging from Homer's *Odyssey,* it took me back to *The Red House*, in particular. I got the feeling that you were going deeper into the seam which you opened in that collection, of engaging with materials which are simultaneously difficult and painful, but also necessary. Making art can operate as a form of camera obscura or reflecting glass. By creating distance, and containment, the works produced may enable us to look at, and engage emotionally with, very challenging subject matters with a degree of agency and safety. Has that been part of your process as an artist?

SD: I'm spending a lot of time considering poetics and

my own poetic development presently. It could be a lockdown reflex, we have been forced to think about ourselves in unexpected ways. And when I look back I see that *Red House* was the collection where I began to weave my own self more fully into an assiduously learnt and practised lyric tradition. It seems to me there are different parts to writing poetry. I see this as the visual simile of an electrical circuit, and when all the parts come into contact the circuit is completed, the current can pass through. The parts I have been particularly focused on are (firstly) a sense of self, and (secondly) a stretching outward, a radiating interest in mysteries outside the soul; akin to how Keats describes negative capability as being when 'a man is capable of being in uncertainties, Mysteries, doubts, without any irritable reaching after fact & reason'.

In fact, I realised quite late in my writing life that I lacked the first and most important part, the sense of a whole self; a point from which to begin. So rather than beginning from silence and inarticulacy, as you described, I began from noise, but it wasn't my noise, it was the deafening noise of languages and traditions.

Deformations is in many ways the product of this slow realisation. A way of eliding lived experience and myth, bringing a noisy tradition and an absence into alignment. I've spoken about how the character Pitysad, who is also Odysseus, was a way of writing about PTSD (his name contains the abbreviation). The sequence had its roots in a number of encounters, but most memorably in a conversation with a historian of the nineteenth century about the men who fought in the Napoleonic Wars. I wondered how that generation had coped with PTSD after their experiences of the bloody battlefields of Europe. He said quite seriously that they didn't have PTSD, it didn't exist. I probed further: did he mean that it wasn't named or described? No, he said, it didn't exist. They just got up, dusted themselves off and carried on. I believe he is wrong, and that it was a named and charted phenomenon by this point – the French physician Philippe Pinel describes the effect of post traumatic neurosis on witnesses of the French revolution. But the idea that PTSD is a sort of modern 'snowflake affliction' lingers on distressingly in popular understanding, and prevents us from seeing the underbelly of history; we only see its gleaming mythic scales. We see the survivors and not the cost of surviving.

AH: I value that investigation and witnessing, which you have said before includes material from serving military personnel. Living with PTSD, as a result of my childhood experiences, I can testify that it is a condition which can be made more visible and comprehensible through the medium of language, to the relief of many. In the poem 'remnants/ *silvae',* I interleave my own voice with loose translations of the Latin poet Statius to address PTSD at both a societal and an individual level. While Statius observes "always the mountain top/ threatens us with death", I specify "a body remembers/ in the only language available". At 41 words, including its title, I wanted the poem to have a torn, compressed quality of intermingled reticence and disclosure, mimicking also how trauma may cause PTSD to infiltrate our neurological landscapes and embed itself within them. Your Odysseus/ Pitysad is necessarily altered, in body and mind. I wondered how he, and the subject of the *Odyssey,* first came to you?

SD: I didn't choose the *Odyssey*, it chose me. I had been considering the Eric Gill frieze in the Midland Hotel: 'Odysseus welcomed from the sea by Nausicaa'. I'd been considering it, of course, in the light of Gill's abuse of his daughters. But as I read and reread the book of the *Odyssey* describing this encounter I grew more and more uneasy. This was not a moment of generous hospitality, but a weird honey trap set up by a god. In the end I wrote this moment into a deformed ballad, a form I've sometimes used as a playful way of undercutting the autonomy and the single narrative perspective of the ballad.

After that I wrote the sequence which became 'Pitysad'. It's anti-mythical in every single way and filled with reflecting glass and oblique lines; with doubts and dreams and failures. It's also packed with references to other works. I did this quite deliberately, because I thought: the *Odyssey* stands at the head of a canon, and so I have to write a piece that pulls its canon along behind it. I want to say, though, that I don't consider Odysseus or his men to be inhuman. I think war is inhuman, and humans pass through its fires, and are changed.

I don't mind saying that I could only have written *Deformations* at this point in my life. The sort of wisdom I'd like to have in life, and in poetry, is the lived sort, just as the beauty of your work, Alice, is the rarest sort of beauty, the beauty of survival.

For years I felt I was blundering around in the dark. I knew I was doing the only thing I could be doing, but I had been doing it numbly. Distancing, a sort of emotional holding back from the material, has been built into my approach to the poems. I see this in your work, too. There's a sense of both a very deep engagement and an utter repudiation. So a poet is both re-living in the writing, and at the same time refusing, casting off and stepping away from the experience. In your case it gives the words a hard glittery quality, as if they are both the digging implements and the archaeological finds. Is this a feeling you recognise?

AH: That's a wonderful analogy. Thank you. For me, self-distancing is inextricably part of art-making. I think that is why I reached for the image of the *camera obscura.* European artists used them from the sixteenth century to project landscapes upside down onto a page, to capture them accurately. They have also been used to study eclipses for millennia, making it possible to observe the sun without looking directly at it.

I think that as artists we need to be of and within the source whose energies engender our work, whether or not it emerges directly from our own lived experience. But we also need to separate ourselves from its rawness, and cauterise some of the connections, to find how best to let the material speak. This separation also confers a measure of protection on the creator, given that we have to go in and in again, through successive revisions, to meet an energy which may be very difficult to hold, emotionally, and aesthetically. At the same time, there's inevitably a degree of psychic dissonance in this splitting. It engenders the warp field of instability that allows the work to come alive.

SD: Your work is very tough – necessarily so, because of the experiences it deals with, but there is a joy in it, at least I found a joy in the writing, the moments of striking beauty and tenderness. I hesitate to reach for parallels but I did think of Paul Celan at times and the idea of a possible purification through language. You reach a perfection of pared-back narrative in poems such as 'phare d'ailly'. And related to that question: how much do you work on poems like this one? I puzzled over it, wondering whether it was the surest of sketches or a very worked-over sculpture. Sometimes there's no perceptible difference for the beholder, and of course it hardly matters. It's not an impudent curiosity, I hope, but I am interested, because it's such an achievement:

phare d'ailly

papa the tide at vasterival was going out
when you were carried from our flat as I slept

your jaw swung
open like a latchless door

AH: Thank you Sasha. I'll answer the last part of this question first, if I may. In terms of the shorter poems, they mostly arrive slowly, over time, sometimes out of the discarded masses of longer sequences. I let what I have sit printed on the page, and come back to it, maybe months, or even a year later, as it gradually resolves itself into a balanced shape. I can't force this. There are several poems I couldn't finish in time for *bird of winter,* perhaps because they didn't belong to that sequence. Part of my editing process is to create space for the reader. What the second consciousness brings is as important to the action of the poem, as what the page initially holds. In their intersection, transfiguration can take place.

Turning to your query about beauty and tenderness – I wanted them to be present in the work, not least because I am speaking at times of and for a very young child, whose selfhood was lost to me for decades. When I wrote of the places and people that she/I loved – the grandmother or bonne maman, the Normandy beach below her house, the lost papa – their joyousness needed to be palpable. They were, and are, so resonant for me. I wanted the reader to be nurtured by them, and to find in them moments of shelter from the harsher poems, which directly address the sexual abuse and its consequences.

What distilled the manuscript, and delivered its title, were two five day visits I made in the summer and then autumn of 2019 to Dieppe, with the funding I received from an Arts Foundation Futures award. I was able to paddle on the sands where I paddled with my papa, and see again the colour of the seaweed. At night, the Phare d'Ailly striped the sky with fingers of light. That gave me the charge of positive energy I needed to rally myself, and gather the material together into its alternations of darkness and illumination, injury and healing.

Turning to childhood in your own work, *Deformations'* opening poem, 'Girl and Hare', calls to mind Nabokov's *Lolita,* featuring a girl lying on her "sunlounger...little and freckled". But unlike Lolita, this girl lies with her pet hare beside her, in harmony with, and in possession of, her own animal nature. Both of their aliveness, and vulnerabilities, are caught in the hare's "thin skin, thrown hurriedly over bone and tendon", and its "narrow breast", "rosed with fur,/ and little childish shoulders." As I read further into *Deformations*, it seemed increasingly to me that we were given, as readers, this moment of wholeness as an amulet to hold against the darkness which follows, but also an intactness which the subsequent poems repeatedly break into. Could you say something about 'Girl and Hare', and more generally how vulnerability and strength may sit alongside each other?

SD: Yes! I'm so pleased you asked about 'Girl and Hare' because it is a moment of innocence and balance. I wasn't thinking of Lolita when I wrote it (although Lolita on her sunlounger is an iconic image). The hare is also of course very different from the child, and there's a slight premonition, a hint of threat with his forearms as strong as a man's, but the hare is just a hare and will always be a hare. I'd like to write more about animals. I see you have the motif of a Pompeiian dog running through *bird of winter*. Animals can be a shortcut to real feeling: love, sadness, anger, which are made complex by proximity to humans. I'd like my next collection to be about man and beast – and in a sense that poem, 'Girl and Hare', was the first poem of this next collection.

AH. Ithaca, my dog, has just come to rub her silky head against my hand as I write this, and nudge my fingers with the side of her mouth. She and I both agree with what you say about animals' ability to take us straight into the real. I think they can also be sites of the inexpressible – which is part of what we are moving towards in the process of art-making. In *bird of winter,* the Pompeian dog as a conduit to my bodily self, and different birds as an emblems of my spirit self, were integral to the energies of the work. They gave me places where the 'bestiality' and 'death-force' of sexual abuse could be registered – but also resisted, through resurgences into sound and movement.

Turning back to your work, Sasha, the injuries occasioned by sexual abuse are central to the poems of the first, 'Welfare Handbook' section of *Deformations.* 'One X for Mary and XX for May' works with some of the codes Gill used in his diaries to record sexual intercourse with different women and children in his household and entourage. Creating a moving arrowhead composed of

X's and dashes, your poem brings to the page something which is simultaneously visually beautiful – and intellectually and emotionally appalling. If you try to read it out loud, the phonic sounds create a repetition of the word 'sex' "– XX X XX X XX X", as if the unsayable is finally being said. I wondered how this poem came into being, and also the 'Welfare Handbook' project more generally?

SD. 'Welfare Handbook' is a sequence about the letter cutter and artist Eric Gill, and I delighted in making sure that the sequence was as visually arresting as I could make it. The XXXs were a terrible thing to typeset because I gave them a sort of fairisle pattern and a funny little floating phallic shape. I wanted the shape to make the reader laugh at the warping of Gill's sexual encounters into a typesetter's folly – and so dispel the authority of the abuser. Although even in the laughter there's a sort of shock. That sequence was very hard to write and is hard to read back even, but giving it a visual presence was vital as it needed to serve as the waving of a tattered flag of defiance.

Let's talk about *bird of winter* as a visual book. Is there something intrinsic to these difficult subjects, abuse and the trauma stemming from abuse, which favours the intra-genre approach? Is lyric poetry too marked by its heritage? Is it no longer fit-for-purpose? Does it need tearing apart into its un-constituent parts? I wondered all those things as I read 'cyclical':

cyclical/ *wall painting house of the ceii*

spring
yellow as a
chick my easter shorts
cut wire where her
beak pulped

winter
each night
the hammer breaks
my windows to make
tears fall on the
fresh snow

summer
the sheets
of fear hang clean
from my hands when
the wind blows they
dance

autumn
herbaceous borders
uncover wriggly roots day-mummy
driving the fork night-mummy
pressing my neck

a panther pounces at rams
running from her by a lake

AH: 'cyclical' is a construction of four segments which exists in refraction with a wall painting from a courtyard garden in Pompeii, illustrated in the catalogue *Life and Death in Pompeii and Herculaneum* from the British Museum exhibition. The text below the photograph describes the scene as a "chaos of wild animals" who are in continual mutual pursuit. I wanted the fragments of the poem – which record that it is always 'open season' when a child is being abused – to have a visual correlative in the physical world, to anchor their origins in actual events that took place in my vanished childhood and adolescence. By making the word groupings rotate around the page, like the stations of the cross, or the hours on a clock, I ask people to read differently at a literal level. They cannot simply enter the page at the top, and leave politely again at the bottom. Instead, they have to jump off the poem like a turning fairground ride. Writers I love like Susan Howe, or Don Mee Choi, are among those who disrupt conventional typographies and page layouts, to expand what can be registered. In this case, I wanted the powerlessness of the cyclical repetition to make the vast continent of the unsaid somatically present – freighting the limited words.

Part of my ambivalence towards conventional practice derives from my subject matters, but another element arises from the fact that my mind has never been a monolingual space. I grew up between English and French at home, and also some Spanish, and then took on board Italian as a teenager. When you cohabit with several languages, each with their own patterns, sounds and grammatical structures – three of my languages have an intimate and a formal 'you' singular, but English does not – you discover that there can be no single set of rules, or absolute ways of saying things. That hugely expands the possible, as Valzhyna Mort showed us in her magnificent Poetry Society/ University of Liverpool lecture.

You are a much more adept multiple-language-practitioner than I am Sasha, in that you translate brilliantly from the Russian. Your translation of *In Memory of Memory* by Maria Stepanova was absolutely the best thing that came to me in February 2021, absorbing and sustaining both at once. I wondered if I could close our conversation by asking you about when Russian entered your life, and how it inflects your creative identity and output as an artist?

SD. I share your ambivalence about cultural conventions, and your sense that form is not a stable concept. I began properly speaking Russian at a very formative moment in my childhood and lived in Russia for a long time in the nineties, a period of upheaval in the post-Soviet region. Because we learn languages in context, and by borrowing words from other speakers, the process gives speakers of more than one language a bird-like soul, always in motion. I began writing poetry seriously in Russia, and so my own work was inevitably coloured by the context of a culture which was alternately homely and strange. The linguist knows that personality is defined by linguistic context and we are different people in the different spaces of the languages we know well. If we're inclined to think about this at all, then the question of whether we have any integrity gnaws away at us. Speakers of many languages are also barometers of the commonplaces of human experience and they feel instinctively when these are eroded and disappear: their mobile souls no longer have a place to alight.

These questions are metaphysical, but they have a political complexion if the cultures that serve as homes have different standings in the world, as Don Mee Choi so eloquently demonstrates in her work. In my case the Russia I made myself linguistically manifest in (an odd phrase but it captures what I mean) was a place of disruption, poverty and deficit. An empire had apparently disappeared and history had apparently stopped, but people kept going in a vacuum, carrying out their day-to-day tasks as all the meaning seeped out of their lives. Some of the detail of Pitysad's travels was taken from the travelling I did in that strange half-lit period around a derelict world in which war and displacement were recent memories *and* ever-present threats – turmoil in stasis. The disused ski resort, for example, and the night trains filled with *chelnoki*, the small traders who operated across borders, or the veterans who begged or collected bottles with their war medals pinned to their jackets – I observed all of these as a very young woman, and was changed by them.

I feel a great affinity with my friend, the writer Maria Stepanova. We are the same generation, but for her the movement begins in Russia and reaches outwards. *In Memory of Memory* is a book which binds a family history in the *hortus clausus* of Soviet Russia into the weave of international history and culture. So when I began translating her work it felt in some ways like a mirror image of the direction of own life. We all come from a badly-mended Europe. It's only now that I see how bound I am to the consciousness of that tormented continent.

AH: Thank you so much for those insights, Sasha. Carrying within my own family the aftermath of the genocides of the Shoah, and speaking and reading languages whose literatures describe the European experiences of the twentieth century, I recognise what you say. I am immensely grateful for your work as a translator opening voices into new languages – and as a poet, showing us the world differently.

Four Poems

SEAN O'BRIEN

Lord Back-End

The gabardine. The belt of twine. Brown paper
poking from the trouser-cuffs. Those rings
like knuckledusters, and the wand of bone that steers
an entourage of frosty air. You've been outflanked.
Now all fall down for Lord Back-End.
You that were gold shall be brought low
and you who governed dig your graves –
proverbial, it must be true –
the ring of pick-axes and spades on iron ground
is everywhere inside these woods.
Perhaps you haven't listened. See, a moment
seals the stream in ice upon a lip of stone.
Your moon-white face is there among the fish.
You must have missed the toadstools, then,
who having grown into themselves
like Arcimboldos of deformity
renounced this world and turned to slime.
And the crow falling out of the tree
in a bundle of rags, with no last words,
No hesitation. Doesn't bounce.
Lord Back-End sees, and it is good.
He pokes it with his stick. But as for you,
are you still here, and if so why?

Runners

The elegant women who run with their dogs
through the graveyard, where have they been before now?
They are so self-possessed, yet too preoccupied
with elsewhere and with afterwards to be
entirely present. To be forty-odd and run like that
seems close to immortality. They glide on
through the sunlit pools between the lime-trees,
down to where the tunnelled shade begins
among the older tombs, with ironwork
and obelisks and disregarded claims
to time's attention. There they pause, perhaps,
to take a call, or block one. They must have it
all to do, like emissaries
from a new creation, one that like our own
is taken up with its supreme particulars.

I wish that we could be each other's witnesses,
that I could be the past for you, and you for me,
this moment when the cherry-branch
unsleeves its ice-pink trumpery
and turns to dying, while the blackbirds pick
dispassionately among the stones
to pass the time, as though this morning's
not the thing itself, the first hot day,
but instead a late revision of the future
playing out in real time, able to predict
our chances to the second,
only somehow set aside, like good advice
that in the moment of its giving
wears its welcome out.
                              I see you
pause before the tunnel's mouth, your phones aloft
like failing torches, and I see your dogs,
so loving and so eager for the off,
and now you see them too and smile
and glide away into the dark.

Woodworks

for the chatelaine

Crows
The sitting tenants of the hilltop
keep a weather eye on everything.
Oh, they've heard it all before.
Surprise us, they say. Go on. Thought not

Leaf-storm
At dusk the woods are hurrying away,
clutching all they can carry –
time to be gone. It is over again -
except for the rowan, who stands
wearing only the gale and her earrings.

Ferns
Gamboge before brown
and then done to a crisp,

the ferns lie down, forgetting
summer. This is sleep,

it is sleep, says the goddess
passing through, her blue gown

pressed and cool and brisk
as any Englishwoman

taking charge at need. It is sleep
whose words are once more

ceasing to be words. Lie down
among the ferns now. Sleep.

Stones

Under the snow, where the pub used to stand,
a loathsome pond has settled in,
and down on its bed of asbestos and pipework
the stones are perfectly at home.

The little bastards live for this – the iron earth,
with the plate-glass water like a vitrine
in 'a private collection'. Listen carefully
and you may hear them clench with joy.

No voices here. No opinions. The white field
narrow and long and unloved. Birds
at a pinch – one rook and one magpie
to set the thing off. Monochrome,
as stones apparently prefer. Think of them
rubbing their no-hands together. Job done.

'I'm the last Jewish intellectual'

DAVID HERMAN

Timothy Brennan, *Places of Mind: A Life of Edward Said* (Bloomsbury) £25.00

I was taught by Edward W. Said at Columbia University for a year, 1980–81. Said was then at the height of his career. He had just published his masterpiece, *Orientalism* (1978), a huge influence on what became known as post-colonial criticism. He had been at Columbia since 1963. His great ambition, he told me, was to have Lionel Trilling's office at Columbia. Trilling had died just a few years before, in 1975, and was the grand old man of literary criticism not just at Columbia but in post-war America.

Then there was Said's political reputation. He had just published his first book on Palestinian politics, *The Question of Palestine* (1979), was writing a new book, *Covering Islam* (1981) and had been elected as an independent member of the Palestine National Council. Reagan had just been elected and Said was becoming increasingly interested in writing about networks and affiliations of power, the expert and the public role of the intellectual.

Part of an extraordinary new generation of critics and intellectuals which included Harold Bloom, Geoffrey Hartman, Jacques Derrida and Michel Foucault, he was the only one who appeared regularly on British and American TV. No other literary critic wrote as often for newspapers and magazines. He was that rate thing, a media don who was also acknowledged to be a leading public intellectual.

In the early 1980s Said was immersing himself in Western Marxism. In his seminars he taught Lukács, Gramsci, Raymond Williams and the British New Left. It is hard to overestimate the importance of this group of thinkers on his thinking during the late 1970s and early 1980s as he started to move from French Theory to what he called 'certain kinds of anti-Second International Marxism', in particular where cultural criticism met Marxism. Tim Brennan and I both attended these seminars. For someone who had just graduated from Cambridge, as I had, or from the University of Wisconsin, as Brennan had, this was heady stuff.

Curiously, Brennan gives little flavour of Said as a teacher, especially given that he later became Brennan's doctoral supervisor. His book is clearly written, full of insights and he has interviewed almost a hundred people who knew Said. The basic narrative of Said's life and career is clear, from his birth in Jerusalem in 1935 to his college years at Princeton and Harvard, his discovery of French Theory and politicisation in the Sixties, his turn to Post-Colonialism and then perhaps the most interesting twist of all, right at the end of his life. He was constantly on the move, intellectually *and* politically, and Brennan often does a good job of following the key twists and turns.

But everywhere there are questions and often there are errors, big and small. The book is guilty of political bias, unargued assertions, leaving out important people, events and references and, worst of all, just getting things wrong.

Some of the errors are minor. Vico (1668–1744) was not 'a contemporary' of de Sade (1740–1814); *The Country and the City* was not 'about eighteenth- and early nineteenth-century English rural life as seen through the prism of country-house poems'; Elvis Costello and the Police were not '"me decade" pop music icons'; a TV programme he appeared on with Raymond Williams and Julia Kristeva was not shown in 1986 and was shown on Channel 4 not the BBC; Brennan writes of 'a film he produced for BBC Television's Channel 4' – Channel 4 is not part of the BBC; The Reith Lectures were not 'founded by Bertrand Russell'. And so on.

Then there are bigger errors of judgment. Brennan writes that *Orientalism* 'seemed less and less to fit the prevailing mood' and that 'the cultural Left in the university seemed stalled' at the time. But this was the very moment when the Left was on the rise in universities on both sides of the Atlantic. Fredric Jameson taught at Yale, Said at Columbia, Tony Judt, Gareth Stedman Jones, Raymond Williams and John Barrell at Cambridge; Stuart Hall, Raymond Williams, EP Thompson, EJ Hobsbawm and *The New Left Review* were at their height; Alexander Cockburn and Christopher Hitchens, both then on the Left, constantly attacked Reagan and American foreign policy in South and Central America. This was crucial to the impact of *Orientalism* and Said's later work as a critic and as a public intellectual.

Brennan quotes Said, 'I don't believe in politicizing the classroom,' and then adds 'and not even his detractors could deny it.' Said, he writes, 'took the view that the university should be a refuge from politics...' But in his graduate seminar in 1980 Said taught only texts by Marxists such as Lukács, Gramsci, and Raymond Williams and Brennan himself writes, 'Between 1978 and 1982, his seminars oscillated between a course on British postwar Marxist thinkers (including Eric Hobsbawm, VG Kiernan, and JD Bernal...) and a seminar dedicated to Gramsci and Lukacs.'

Brennan refers to Said teaching Perry Anderson's essay, *Components of the National Culture* about 'the deadening effects on British culture of the wave of conservative intellectual immigrants to the UK after World War II (among them, Karl Popper, Lewis Namier, and Ludwig Wittggenstein).' But Wittgenstein, Isaiah Berlin (a key figure in the same Anderson essay) and Namier came to Britain before the war and Wittgenstein and Namier were both influential between the wars.

Then there is the political bias. Brennan is clearly on the Left and it is always clear where his sympathies lie. The book is dedicated 'For the Palestinian people.' He writes of 'the October war' in 1973. If he called it the Yom Kippur War it would mean acknowledging that Israel was attacked on the most holy day of the Jewish year.

Brennan has little time for those he considers on the Right. He dismisses 'Cold War writers for hire like Arthur Koestler' or writers who take a different view of the post-colonial world from Said, like V.S. Naipaul. Both were major writers and deserve better than this. Christopher Hitchens is attacked for 'pretending to correct Said's "errors"'. He didn't pretend and he pointed out serious errors which Brennan does not attempt to refute. Hitchens made the argument unlike Brennan who puts the word errors in inverted commas as if that wishes them away. Nor is there any mention of Hitchens's long-time friendship with Said or that they co-wrote a book on the Palestinians before they fell out. There is no reference to Ernest Gellner's review of *Culture & Imperialism* in the *TLS* but he is simply dismissed by Brennan as Said's 'old nemesis'. Conrad, a hugely important writer for Said, is at one point dismissed as 'the politically dubious Conrad'. This is just name-calling.

Too often Brennan relies on Left-wing intellectuals for their views. 'The historian Perry Anderson believed it the finest statement on the pernicious term "terrorist" to be found anywhere.' He approvingly quotes Seymour Hersh and Israel Shahak as if they are impartial observers. He knows they were long-time critics of American foreign policy and Israel.

Brennan's language can be slippery. He writes of 'the pernicious term "terrorist"'. Is it? He writes of 'a mania like Orientalism' and 'philologist-scoundrels.' Was it a 'mania'? Were they 'scoundrels'?

Then there are loose assertions. How does he know what was chanted at Said's birth? More important, he is surprisingly vague about when exactly the Said family moved from Jerusalem to Cairo, which he must know is a hugely controversial question which has been fiercely debated since Said published his memoir, *Out of Place*

(1999). Jerusalem, Brennan writes, was 'the site of his birth and baptism, of frequent family pilgrimage and early schooling' but 'Cairo was Said's childhood anchor all the same.' 'Pilgrimage' and 'anchor' seem to be doing a lot of work here. 'Jerusalem might have been the homeland but was never home.' 'Might'? We are given dates for Said's schools in Cairo but not for his time at St. George's in Jerusalem.

There is a controversial article challenging Said's claims to be a Palestinian refugee by Justus Reid Weiner, "My Beautiful Old House and Other Fabrications by Edward Said" *(Commentary*, September 1999). Weiner is not mentioned in the Index. In a book of almost five hundred pages Brennan gives only three paragraphs to criticising the article. You would expect Brennan to refute it in detail. He doesn't.

At school in America in the early 1950s, writes Brennan, 'Said was already known as a passionate partisan of the Palestinian cause'. But five pages later, he was 'by his own account apolitical.' Later, on a very different issue, Brennan writes, 'Said's reading in phenomenology, existentialism, and psychoanalysis was extensive, but his allegiances were skin-deep.' 'Extensive' or 'skin-deep'?

Then there are important moments which barely register or are missing altogether. In 1966 Said attended the famous conference at Johns Hopkins on 'The Languages of Criticism and the Sciences of Man'. Everyone who was anyone in the new world of French Theory was there. For the rest of the Sixties and Seventies, Said became known as a key figure in the arrival of Post-Structuralism in America, confirmed by his breakthrough book, *Beginnings* (1975). But the conference barely merits two pages.

'Literary Theory changed Said forever,' Brennan writes. He is right. Literary Theory but also continental philosophy. During his early years at Columbia, Said wrote essays on Lucien Goldmann, Merleau-Ponty, Poulet, Lévi-Strauss, E.M. Cioran, the young Lukács and Nietzsche. He reinvents himself as a critic, finding a new Continental voice. This raises an interesting question. To what extent was Said a follower of fashion? In the 1950s, writes Brennan, he read about phenomenology, existentialism and psychoanalysis. All were fashionable at the time. Then he writes a PhD on Conrad (1964, published 1966). He was, writes Brennan astutely, 'Clever enough to realize he would be more likely to succeed professionally by writing a conventional study of a canonical English author.' Then Said embraces Literary Theory. This is what makes his name. Brennan focuses on the big French names: Barthes, Derrida, Foucault. But there are only two references to Geoffrey Hartman and to J. Hillis Miller, one to Paul de Man, none to Spivak. Said then moves on in less than twenty years to *Orientalism* (1978) and post-colonialism. But then after *Culture and Imperialism* (1993) he is on the move again in the last years of his life.

Why this constant movement? In his Introduction to the fiftieth anniversary edition of Auerbach's *Mimesis*, Said writes, 'he exudes a sense of searching and discovery.' This is also true of Said. He had an enormous appetite for ideas. He was an essayist. No dusty academic monographs for him. At the same time, there was a handful of important writers and thinkers who stayed with him throughout his career. He once called Conrad, 'a steady groundbass to much that I have experienced.' He was not only the subject of Said's PhD, he was also one of the central figures in *Beginnings*, an important figure in *Culture and Imperialism* and *Reflections on Exile* and the subject of several important essays. He is rightly one of the key figures in Brennan's book. Said was loyal to Conrad and others but also constantly on the move. Ambition and opportunism, going where the action was? Or just hungry for new ideas, wide-ranging in his interests? Not for the first time, Brennan isn't drawn to these big questions about his subject.

Was Said an outsider at Columbia when he first arrived in the 1960s? It's hard to tell because there is very little in *Places of Mind* on Lionel Trilling, nothing on Diana Trilling, two references to Steven Marcus, three to his close friend, Michael Wood (including nothing on Wood's brilliant review of *Culture & Imperialism* in *The New York Review of Books*, which at more than 6000 words would be hard to miss).

Was Said an outsider in 1980s and '90s America? Brennan thinks so. Said 'had become a pariah among the pro-Israel wing of New York publishing,' he writes. But Said was a regular contributor to *Grand Street*, *The Nation,* wrote numerous op-ed pieces for *The Guardian* and the *New York Times,* from 1981 he wrote almost fifty articles for *The London Review of Books,* he wrote on his Cairo childhood in *House & Garden* and on Arafat for Andy Warhol's *Interview*. He appeared regularly on the key news and current affairs programmes as a spokesman for the Palestinians and appeared in talks programmes and on TV documentaries on BBC2 and Channel 4. One of the most famous literary critics in America, he became President of the Modern Languages Association and gave prestigious lectures such as the 1993 Reith Lectures, The TS Eliot Lectures in 1985, The Wellek Library Lectures at UC Irvine, The Empson Lectures at Cambridge University, The Lionel Trilling Lectures at Columbia University, The Henry Stafford Little Lectures at Princeton and lectures at the Collège de France. 'A pariah'?

Orientalism was arguably Said's most influential book. Few critics have opened up a whole cultural landscape in the way he did. It had its critics as well as its admirers. Brennan doesn't engage with them, he just dismisses them: 'Few critics bothered to reckon with any of Said's philosophical points of departure,' 'his detractors were puzzled, unused to dealing with such complexities,' 'their criticisms often missed their mark,' 'None of these critics, though, knew anything at all about Said's earlier work or how that related to *Orientalism*.'

It's hard to know whether these claims are remotely true because they hardly get discussed. Robert Irwin and Jacques Berque get three mentions, Bernard Lewis and David Stern two, Daniel Martin Varisco appears on two pages. Sometimes the mentions seem like put-downs: Varisco is introduced as 'an anthropological expert on thirteenth-century Yemeni agricultural texts' and Irwin as 'a medieval specialist on the Mamluks.' This follows a pattern. When people criticise Said for his politics or his scholarship, there is little engagement. They are simply dismissed. It's the same whether it's Weiner's attack on Said's memoir, Ernest Gellner's review of *Culture & Imperialism* or Bernard Lewis's 7,465-word essay on *Orientalism* in *The New York Review of Books* (just one reference by Brennan).

Most important of all are the absences. Brennan writes in some detail about Said's lack of engagement with Marx, psychoanalysis and especially feminism. The last point is perhaps the most interesting. Said's pantheon was almost entirely male. His favourite poets were Cavafy and Hopkins, Conrad and Swift were major figures throughout his career, his favourite thinkers and critics included Lukács, Gramsci and Vico, Auerbach, Spitzer and Adorno, Raymond Williams, Foucault and Fanon; long-time friends and colleagues included Chomsky, Hitchens, Alex Cockburn and Israel Shahak, Eqbal Ahmad, IF Stone, John Berger and Jean Mohr, Ben Sonnenberg, Sami Al-Banna and Daniel Barenboim, Kamal Nasser, Ibrahim Abu-Lughod and Bayan Al-Hout. All men. Political philosophers or literary critics, journalists or Palestinian activists, the pattern seems the same.

Brennan can be insightful about Said's inner life: his experience of clinical depression and insomnia, his love of expensive clothes and his astonishing appetite for work. But there are also aspects of Said's personality which seem to elude him. Of almost one hundred interviewees most are men. And when they make it into the book, these women hardly feature. Only female relatives are mentioned more than five times. What did the other women have to say?

Much of Brennan's best work has been on post-colonialism, an area opened up by Said. So, it is perhaps surprising that there is so little about other leading post-colonial critics, historians and writers. There is almost nothing on Ranajit Guha and the Subaltern Studies Group, Gayatri Spivak and Homi K. Bhabha, R. Siva Kumar, CLR James or Aimé Césaire. Brennan gives the impression that Said was more interested in Palestinian and Arab culture than in post-colonial literature but Césaire, Fanon, Guha and CLR James are all significant presences in *Culture & Imperialism*.

Most surprising of all is the near absence of Salman Rushdie and especially *The Satanic Verses*. There are four references to Rushdie, none of which are to *The Satanic Verses* or the *fatwa*. But Rushdie reviewed Said's book, *After the Last Sky* in *The Guardian*, interviewed Said at the ICA (later published in *The New Left Review* and republished in *Imaginary Homelands*) and Said co-signed a letter to *The New York Review of Books* in March 1989 condemning 'the vilification, book banning and threats of physical violence against Salman Rushdie, the gifted author of *Midnight's Children, Shame*, and *The Satanic Verses*.' The letter, an important statement by a number of leading post-colonial academics concludes, 'we reaffirm our belief in universal principles of rational discussion and freedom of expression.' None of this is mentioned by Brennan.

What would have become of Said had he lived longer? In particular, how would he have coped with the climate of growing intolerance and political correctness in American universities? Said, was tolerant and open to debate. He abhorred censorship. He would definitely have been against the current in today's 'cancelling'

culture. Towards the end of his career he was opposed, writes Brennan, to the new vanguard 'that to him had thrown out some of the most critical thinking of the past on the grounds that it was white and male.' He was 'at odds with the drift of academic fashions, he taught less as the decade wore on, complaining that students had lost their critical sense and were unable to take a position.' In just three pages towards the end, Brennan creates a fascinating image of an embattled, increasingly isolated Said.

It is also curious that Brennan gives so little attention to some of Said's best essays, including 'Secular Criticism', 'Traveling Theory' (both mentioned once) and 'Contra Mundum' (his brilliant review in *The London Review of Books* of E.J. Hobsbawm's *Age of Extremes*, republished in *Reflections of Exile*, but not mentioned by Brennan). Finally, there is a brief reference to a fascinating moment near the end of Said's life which is hugely important. In an interview with Ari Shavit for the Israeli publication, *Ha'aretz*, later republished in *Power, Politics and Culture* (2001), Said told Shavit, 'I'm the last Jewish intellectual. You don't know anyone else. ... I'm the last one. The only true follower of Adorno.'

This is an extraordinary statement coming from the greatest Palestinian intellectual, who spent much of his life debating and writing about Israel and the Middle East. What could Said possibly have meant?

In a fascinating essay, 'A Glorious Achievement: Edward Said and the Last Jewish Intellectual', Professor Bryan Cheyette asks whether this is postmodern playfulness or something darker? He traces some of the references that might have influenced Said. In her Introduction to Walter Benjamin's famous book of essays, *Illuminations*, Hannah Arendt famously called Benjamin, the 'last European'. Jacques Derrida called himself 'the last of the Jews that I still am'. Two 'last Jews' structure Claude Lanzmann's film, *Shoah*: Shimon Srebnik, one of only two survivors of Chelmno, and Simcha Rottem, who thought of himself as the 'last Jew' after the destruction of the Warsaw Ghetto.

There is another clue. One of Susan Sontag's greatest essays was on Walter Benjamin. It was published in *The New York Review of Books* as 'The Last Intellectual' (it was republished as the title essay in *Under The Sign of Saturn*). She writes at the end,

'In his essay on [Karl] Kraus, Benjamin asks rhetorically: "Does Kraus stand on the frontier of a new age? "Alas, by no means. For he stands on the threshold of the Last Judgment." Benjamin is thinking of himself. At the Last Judgment, the Last Intellectual – that saturnine hero of modern culture, with his ruins, his defiant visions, his reveries, his unquenchable gloom, his downcast eyes – will explain that he took many "positions" and defended the life of the mind to the end, as righteously and inhumanly as he could.'

This sounds like Said. He was a great critic and a famous political activist, but there is something else, much stranger, about Said at the end of his life. He took a kind of Jewish turn. He had always been fascinated by the great Jewish German scholars and critics: Erich Auerbach, Leo Spitzer, Benjamin, Adorno and the young Lukács. They were all German-speaking Central Europeans. They were all male. They were all Jews. Most were Marxists. They were all refugees. And they were all part of that extraordinary moment in central European culture when the nineteenth-century gave way to twentieth-century modernism. Finally, they all mattered to Said and some – Lukács, Adorno and Auerbach – were key figures for hm.

At the end it was this group of writers that Said increasingly turned to. In 2000 he delivered the Lionel Trilling Lectures at Columbia University. In their Introduction to *The Selected Works of Edward Said, 1966–2006* (2019), Moustafa Bayoumi and Andrew Rubin write that in these lectures, 'Said brought together three major threads in his work: his long-standing interest in philology (in the work of Erich Auerbach in particular), his deepening engagement with Adorno's work, and his ongoing commitment to humanism.'

In 2003 he published an Introduction to the 50th anniversary edition of Auerbach's *Mimesis* ('its humanistic example remains an unforgettable one') and his lecture, *Freud and the non-European* (2003). In *Musical Elaborations* (1991), he writes that he is 'profoundly indebted' to Adorno who is his chief interlocutor in the book. This debt can be seen specially at the end of *Humanism and Democratic Criticism* (2004). It is what Said later called Adorno's 'contrapuntal voice', which, according to Cheyette, 'enables him to bring together classical music, the intellectual and dispossessed peoples, and humanist critique.'

Deeply pessimistic about the future of the Palestinians, increasingly isolated in the academy, Said turned from literary criticism and political activism to a group of Jewish thinkers and critics, the last Jewish intellectuals – Jews, exiles and in the case of Adorno, passionate about music. There was only one important Jewish figure who was a contemporary of Said's. Daniel Barenboim, with whom he set up The West-Eastern Divan Orchestra and co-wrote, *Parallels and Paradoxes* (2002). These became his last, great themes as he approached death, riddled with leukemia.

It is a tragic end. Brennan's politics blind him to the tragedy and pessimism. They don't allow him to see the full complexity of Said's life and work. He was so much more than a Palestinian activist. Like Walter Benjamin, Said took many positions and 'defended the life of the mind to the end'.

Two Poems

THEODORE ELL

A yield

No cliffs, only a rounding off into the sea.
The pasture slopes and just gives way.
There is this shape along the inlet
where breakers shy from digging at the edge,
though some days they turn.

When I am down there, do not come looking for me.
It is exposed. There is a blame of wind.
And if the turf goes, there is no hitching you back
up from that hem.
For a moment you will have silver waves below your feet,
then it will be all cold noise and traffic.
You are on the verges of a great highway there.

It is where I find myself on the long days of a good season.
You will know them
because I will refuse to come up home
even when you call out the time.
I will be out of earshot, thinking,

Those are the millimetres I must plough.

Generators

I

All patina, dial and pirouettes
the windmill

hovering above the corrugated roof
could be an airman,

standing, arms folded, by a runway,
knees locked in the gale streaming out his scarf,

admiring squadron after squadron
drumroll down to the lift frontier

and reach out in fading half-miles
all afternoon. The windmill,

so new to look at
you never knew which part to look at:

three-sided ladder, sunflower in chains,
face like a second's glare from a locomotive wheel,

slow cards dealing hand from hand
but not into a deck –

a sudden peak above the house
to take eyes off legwork one whole season

and keep McEnultys shaking their heads.
No bore, no pump or axles at its feet,

only the sight, from hills away,
of a stripling in shorts, all silhouettes

he climbed that quick about the scaffold,
wiring the heart of the fans

down a spindle in the middle,
or standing, sometimes, up top, watchful

it seemed, as though lightning could earth
there from a single slow wing of cloud.

Afternoons alone like that, up top.
(He had that way of frowning all through dinner,

piling up salt on his plate rim –
but then, he was off from the University –

no blame if he had thoughts tailing him.)
Then other crates came

on the Merriwa Flyer, the slowest train
in the Hunter, that never delivered firm ice cream,

and he was business all at once
in the shed he'd put up by the kitchen garden,

unpacking the deep black tubs
his diagrams called batteries

that he hooked up
to the cogged-in poles from up top

through just one crossways-spinning silver canister
and the wireless fanfared itself,

the verandas made a lantern of that hilltop
in nights no paraffin had travelled,

way was made for the Kelvinator
that would keep the cream cakes from running.

McEnultys electrified, and no wires out of Merriwa,
the talk of the backgammon boards

in the Fitzroy: Those relics powered up by some
    blow-in.
Say what you like about him, McEnultys said –

he paid his way for those term breaks,
that father of his not wanting the upkeep –

and went on to doctor bombers,
something to do with flying torpedoes, those swarms

the papers showed coming at battleships
out of gauze skies. He didn't give much away –

just kept earning more details for his epaulettes –
and squadrons would think little of him

stood out on the apron,
reading late cirrus, element-red

and corrugating over someone's hills,
propellers nearby idling down – though

there would be the windmill,
engineered, as McEnultys thought,

in his own image.

II

You'd swear it put whole acres
under glass – pasture in medleys, wheat parquet –

that microscope.
Every tick-over of a lens-piece

shows a map, an inlaid scene
in raw material.

Gridlock the colour of dry in a grass blade.
Channels and wells across red plains

in blood made flat under the coverslip,
the pin-end a looming pencil.

Nothing she won't trial,
jabbing her thumb

or picking up snakeskin
by the back step, to read dioramas

atlases only abridge.
Nor a minute missed

between finishing ice cream
(hard as teeth

but it will be years
till McEnultys have a gentler freezer)

and sitting up in the bureau chair
before bedtime, bowed to the eyepiece

as the eyepiece bows to the slide.
Sandalled feet past halfway to the floor.

Torchlight only, mostly cupped
in the mirror that fingers steer,

though the remainder
dimly includes her.

A smallholding at dusk
in a far region

of the long front room. Chills and loose wainscoting,
a night of the house's own.

Bedtime grows later
as McEnultys come to her, caller

by diffident caller,
knowing the hours but with a mind to let her be

(Let her, we ought to, they nod
over the china, her father might know aeroplanes

but there's nothing he'll do with her)
then stooping into the light, at her offer,

to gaze into a moth wing:
hairline creeks plotting shade for miles.

It's no dream she's looking into
but the maker's mark, McEnultys nod

into their chins. A pulse of rosary beads.
In these stays, handed on

from home, she's been used to seeing things dead –
that wether in the chute pen

coughing and pitched over
like it wanted to chafe its back off

and the rest trying to flee,
shuddered several thick at the rails,

a winded bag, legs rigid, all that's left
in the dirt ring –

though the microscope,
its fearful weight

newly handed down with ribbons and applause,
is telling of sources.

It's starting to seem there's company.
Dumb-useless, father calls that

before silence comes back into his face,
you go to Merriwa

till you grow a brain in your head.
It isn't him she'll think of

when she tilts the bottle and the calf drinks finally
that she's wrenched from deep inside

a stranded mother,
but grandsire McEnulty

in his threadbare crimson gown
taking up the doorway

and beckoning her quietly in again,
telling her, voice like flyscreen hinges,

never to get old – down the long front room:
dust-cloth, frost on windows,

lamplight on the little mauve and emerald panes
with their backs to the night air –

Never get old, girl.

III

A hole in brightness, a deletion
from dazed fields,

the shade inside an opened oil barrel
on a gate-pole:

a letterbox
not a word reaches,

just return airlifts
of the brown-papered doves

posting twigs into it
or inspecting the sky from the slot,

their cornerless hangar,
their apartment in the plains.

Cracked enamel, lichening rust,
wind in the dented aperture,

the name of McEnulty
in grey and separating wood

hung from pinched eye-hooks:
the letterbox,

the fixture
of cold morning vacancies

when lone tree-shadows
whiten the soil

and the parallel foot-trails
dotting acres of crystals

belong to the siblings,
meandering

through the sleep frontier
for small treasure

(have the tenants delivered
in the armoured nest

among the pale castoff-feathers?),
out from crumpled eaves,

a grey veranda.
There, walled in distance,

the living Miss McEnulty in her dark wool-cords
sighs into bent wicker,

blows steam off fogged tea, waits
as her other guest peels sheets

off trenched mattresses: the sleeve-rolled mother
of those two (who hardly need watching after

though it's a change
to see something moving in the mornings).

A girl for whom sprung midday grasses
are limbering a canter-stride,

a boy who from winter dawn air
is learning the feel of the razor –

a pair who think of grouped eggs
in one greater shell

as familiar and likely (never mind
their mother's harping on the breeding season,

those cells she insists on), who have a way of reckoning
the gist of cross-talk dinners

with glances
replying to glances,

who gather from frowned silence
that the chutes and gated aisles

of the shearers' labyrinth
where they can outrun barred sunlight

may be filled with little else
past these years,

who find a rosary in cracked mud in the dam
where it can only have been thrown –

who wonder how the old lady
beneath the gap-toothed motionless

windmill
could have been born at all,

looking like a mist
will walk off with her,

though what they're told
of when she was new

beneath that spun bullseye
tells them of all births at once.

A crossing in their personhood,
this one memory they can step inside.

Sun, again, as in a lens. Frost
dissolving as spilled salt.

Far up, a chalked line following
minute wingtips,

an arrow in blue silence.
Earthed, these peer selves

at the letterbox: their paired
whispers

turning in the barrel, eye
seeing forethoughts in eye,

then standing at intervals,
humming,

walking from time
to time,

their hill among hills.

Three Poems

JOSHUA WEINER

An Ecology

Dry Maine pine
needle
     dropped
late

Leadbetter's
August afternoon

into the open
spine

– undislodgeable –

of my own

Collected
    hardcover
        Niedecker.

Inkling

Open field. Late sun.
White kite riding the thermals.
In the field, no shadow
and my shadow run.

Even So

11.8.20

So you still have to
    duck & cover,
for the war is still
    not over;
the mind of man is a busy
    butcher,
and civilization
    a state of nature.

Nietzsche's style guide

IAIN BAMFORTH

Nietzsche scribbled down the ten instructions of his 'style guide' for the twenty-one-year-old Lou Salomé during what proved to be the high point of their relationship, an idyllic three weeks spent together (although Nietzsche's disobligingly jealous sister Elisabeth was, as it were, lurking in the undergrowth) in the Thuringian village of Tautenburg, about twenty-five kilometres east of Weimar, in August 1882.

Every morning Nietzsche would knock on Lou's door at the vicarage (he was staying in the farmer's house) and they would set off on a long walk together; on one of these mornings 'F.N.' brought a sheet of paper with him. Before she had come to Tautenburg, Lou had been working on a series of 190 aphorisms ('Stibber Nestbuch'): Nietzsche numbered the best of them, corrected or tightened a score, and put marginalia next to others. Her 'Sometimes the size of our conscience stands in inverse ratio to the size of our brain', for instance, was sharpened to the chiasmatic: 'Big conscience, small brain: often the case.' Angela Livingstone comments on the 'peculiar pathos' of Lou's literary style in her autobiography: 'it is somehow swollen, it is naively sententious, and it is unnecessarily secretive.' Lou had no reservations about accepting Nietzsche's textual advice (she 'could learn to write in a day', he told her), but was uncertain about the exact nature of their relationship. Still implicated in the famous platonic love triangle with Nietzsche's younger colleague Paul Rée, she wrote to Rée that people who saw them on their walks took them for a couple, and feared that Tautenburg would become 'Trautenburg' ('betrothal-burg').

Rhetoric – the whole matter not just of expressing oneself but of adapting the expression of the matter at hand in the presence of a significant other or others – was always important to Nietzsche: his training in and deep-rooted knowledge of classical rhetoric, the art of public speaking, has almost been lost to European education, except perhaps in some of the more conservative French and Italian institutions. A full decade before meeting Lou, Nietzsche in his professorial days in Basel had even sketched the plan of a book to be called *Considerations on Reading and Writing*. He delivered a course on rhetoric during the winter semester of 1872–3 (attended by only two students) that dismissed the popular assimilation of rhetoric to eloquence, and instead developed its dependence on figural language: 'language is itself the result of purely rhetorical tricks and devices...'. Nietzsche would be the first to admit that the modern art of rhetoric, although deferring to the old oral tradition, is, like all other modern 'arts', a product of writing. (This is what he asserts in rule three: know what you want to write before you put it on paper. Know what you want to say before you come out with it.)

Even in the new chirographic structures of thought, the rhetorical tradition – sequentially organised and scientifically structured – has its place. 'Rhetoric cannot simply be disparaged if we can assume that man is predestined to it by his needs. It is not simply the art of demagogic lure; it has also always had its meaning for forms of spiritual care and for the bringing about of a better disposition of mind and greater joy of living...', argued the German philosopher Hans Blumenberg, a century after Nietzsche. 'The fundamental error of all criticism of rhetoric is the assumption that the naked truth that is concealed by it would on its own suffice to cope with what is revealed.'

This art is one of constant adaptation in our interactions with others – a dynamic, social and relational process. Adam Smith's instructions for 'perspicuity' and 'propriety' in his 'Considerations concerning the First Formation of Languages', an essay of 1761, require the speaker to anticipate the effect his words will have on the hearer. By perspicuity Smith means an unadorned style and economy of means – a 'neat, clear, plain and clever manner' – that projects itself while revealing intention: this may be compared to Nietzsche's third rule: 'this is what I want to say and report'. By propriety, Smith means how language *fits*: the speaker's native qualities and intentions as well as the circumstances and qualities of the person addressed. It is an act of anticipation: what effect are my words going to have? Ralph Waldo Emerson, one of the few nineteenth-century writers Nietzsche unreservedly admired, put it similarly (even if he did use that word 'eloquence'): 'Eloquence is the power to translate a truth into language perfectly intelligible to the person to whom you speak'. 'Syncatabasis' – in the intricate rhetorical terminology out of Greek and Latin – is the term for adapting a rhetorical style to the level of the interlocutor, although Nietzsche is astute in recommending a style that suits the writer's needs too. He calls this 'the law of mutual relation'.

We don't have to read very far in Nietzsche's mature works to find observations and recommendations that match the concise rules of his style guide for Lou. Item 188, 'Thinkers as Stylists', in section four of *Menschlich, All-zu-menschlich* (*Human, All Too Human*), runs: 'Most thinkers write badly because they tell us not only their thoughts but also the thinking of their thoughts.' In 'Gait', entry 282 of *Der fröhliche Wissenschaft* (*The Joyful Science*), Nietzsche comments: 'There is something laughable about the sight of authors who enjoy the rustling folds of long and involved sentences: they are trying to cover up their *feet*.' This is a wittier version of his rule six, in which he instructs Lou to be careful of periodic sentences, the kind of convoluted and dangling syntax that most people associate with the German language. But English has its periods too. Matthew Arnold once complained about Milton's introit to *Paradise Lost*: 'So chary of a sentence is he, so resolute not to let it escape him till he has crowded into it all he can, that it is not until the thirty-ninth word in the sentence that he will give us the key to it, the word of action, the verb.'

In 'Why I Write Such Good Books', one of the chapters in his last original book, the parodic autobiography *Ecce Homo*, Nietzsche recapitulates almost word for word his advice to Lou. 'Every style is *good* which accurately communicates an inner condition, which makes no mistake as to the signs, the tempo of the signs, the *gestures* – all rules of phrasing are an art of gesture.' Dumb-show elements are just as important as utterance. This is what he insists in rule five of his style guide, too. Here he contradicts a classical authority: Cicero thought that theatricality was the supreme temptation for the novice orator and therefore to be avoided, although later writers of manuals on speaking skills – Giovanni Bonifacio in his *Art of Signs* (1616), for instance – were persuaded that gesture offers a dimension of agreed sense that ordinary language lacks. Body language, as we would say. It was ironically Gilbert Austin in his *Chironomia* (1806), one of the first works to map the entire gamut of movements of public speaking, who decided that English orators were speaking statues: 'It is not the genius of the people of Great Britain to gesticulate; they are grave people. To saw the air perpetually is absurd.'

In fact, Nietzsche's recommendations would hardly dismay a contemporary advertising copywriter: Nietzsche is the exemplary 'Mad Man'. In the television series of that name, Dan Draper pitches a campaign for Kodak's new circular slide projector which he proposes calling a 'carousel', rightly intuiting that the word will evoke pleasurable childhood memories in prospective customers. We are in the realm of Nietzsche's rule nine. His rule eight might seem to have little application to copywriting, which rarely deals with abstractions, but there is evidence of a perfectly primed sensibility in the l'Oréal catchphrase 'because I'm worth it' (*'parce que je le vaux bien'*): this was coined in 1973 by Ilon Specht, a young NY copywriter who thought it expressed feminist defiance. It now sounds like the entitled demanding another freebie.

There is another reminder of Emerson (and Montesquieu in *De l'esprit des lois*) in Nietzsche's rule ten. In a letter addressed to his friend C. J. Woodbury, Emerson wrote: 'The most interesting writing is that which does not quite satisfy the reader. Try and leave a little thinking for him... A little guessing does him no harm, so I would assist him with no connections.' Assist with no connections: in other words, don't be too logical and predictable, Emerson suggests, since connections will be made one way or other. Think, for instance, of the Adidas slogan: 'Impossible is nothing' which inverts what the angel of the annunciation says to Mary in Luke 1:37: 'For with God nothing shall be impossible'. Good ad copy takes something familiar and makes it strange, strange enough (as it treads on almost completely forgotten religious sensibilities) to hold our attention.

But if we care to dwell on it, one of Nietzsche's most famous lapidary phrases – 'Werde der, der du bist!' ('Become who you are!') – sounds just like an advertising slogan. Nietzsche had a genius for marketing his own brand, even if his exhortation was a quote from Pindar (and adopted by many other writers, if not quite so pith-

ily). Nietzsche knew his tradecraft in and out. He has the rare ability to address himself to the individual reader, to write elegantly if often hyperbolically, to pitch his delivery for maximum impact – above all, he has the master coach's ability to convey the impression that he is writing *just for you*. He must have sensed this ability himself. How else to explain the subtitle he appended to the titlepage of his famous *Zarathustra*: 'For everyone and no one'?

And Lou – who would write about their encounter twelve years later in her biography (and would never lose the wordiness of her prose style) – must also have sensed in Tautenburg that the dry instructions of Nietzsche's style guide were not simply about exhorting her to be a better writer; they were also what the art of classical rhetoric has always been about: *wooing* the intended recipient.

Stillehre für Lou/Style guide for Lou

FRIEDRICH NIETZSCHE

(Tautenburg, August 1882)

Zur Lehre vom Stil/On Style

1. Das Erste, was noth thut, ist Leben: der Stil soll *leben*.	The primordial thing is life: style must be *lively*.
2. Der Stil soll *dir* angemessen sein in Hinsicht auf eine ganz bestimmte Person, der du dich mittheilen willst. (*Gesetz der doppelten Relation*.)	A style should suit *you* in respect of the one person in particular with whom you wish to communicate. (*The law of mutual relation*.)
3. Man muß erst genau wissen: „so und so würde ich dies sprechen und *vortragen*' – bevor man schreiben darf. Schreiben muß eine Nachahmung sein.	You must first know exactly "this is what I want to say and *present*" before you allow yourself to write. Writing must be copy-perfect.
4. Weil dem Schreibenden viele *Mittel* des Vortragenden *fehlen*, so muß er im Allgemeinen eine *sehr ausdrucksvolle* Art von Vortrag zum Vorbild haben: das Abbild davon, das Geschriebene, wird schon nothwendig viel blässer ausfallen.	Since the writer *lacks* many of the speaker's *means*, he must generally have *a very expressive* kind of presentation as a model, since the written version of it is bound to appear much more pallid.
5. Der Reichthum an Leben verräth sich durch *Reichthum an Gebärden*. Man muß Alles, Länge und Kürze der Sätze, die Interpunktionen, die Wahl der Worte, die Pausen, die Reihenfolge der Argumente – als Gebärden empfinden *lernen*.	An abundance of life reveals itself through *abundance of gestures*. You have to *learn* to feel everything as gestures: the length and brevity of phrases, punctuation marks, the choice of words, pauses, how the arguments stack up.
6. Vorsicht vor der Periode! Zur Periode haben nur die Menschen ein Recht, die einen langen Athem auch im Sprechen haben. Bei den Meisten ist die Periode eine Affektation.	Be careful of long sentences! Only people who are long-winded even when talking are entitled to long sentences. With most people, long sentences are an affectation.
7. Der Stil soll beweisen, daß man an seine Gedanken *glaubt*, und sie nicht nur denkt, sondern *empfindet*.	Style ought to demonstrate that you *believe* in your thoughts, and *feel* – not just think – them.
8. Je abstrakter die Wahrheit ist, die man lehren will, um so mehr muß man erst die *Sinne* zu ihr verführen.	The more abstract the truth you wish to teach the more you must first seduce the *sensibility* for it.

9. Der Takt des guten Prosaikers in der Wahl seiner Mittel besteht darin, *dicht* an die Poesie heranzutreten, aber *niemals* zu ihr überzutreten.

10. Es ist nicht artig und klug, seinem Leser die leichteren Einwände vorwegzunehmen. Es ist sehr artig und *sehr klug*, seinem Leser zu überlassen, die letzte Quintessenz unsrer Weisheit *selber auszusprechen*.

F. N.
Einen guten Morgen,
meine liebe Lou!

The sensibility of the good prose writer resides in choosing his means so as to come *close* to poetry but *never* to go over to it.

It is not polite or clever to deprive your reader of the more obvious objections. It is very good manners and *very clever* to allow your reader *alone to pronounce* on whether our wisdom possesses this ultimate quality.

F.N.
Good morning,
my dear Lou!

Three Poems

JANE KING

For a son from another mom

Driving to the airport for your fourth year
at university. Been on this road
a long time. I think I see you quite clearly.

A landmark sparks a memory. A story's spilt.
Your origin story always leaks like this.
My picture of your life's a patchwork quilt.

There is no sequence, just some bursts of snaps.
I know I tried my best to intervene
When I could see you really needed help.

But every tiny horror sparks my guilt
I never really knew how bad it was.
Rounding a bend – vertiginous feelings tilt.

Triolet for all my moody men

I know y'all think I'm soft and can be turned
but take your moody self and walk away.
Remember some things harden when they're burned.
I know y'all think I'm soft and can be turned.
I'm sorry that all now you haven't learned
Because Fuck Off is all I want to say.
I know y'all think I'm soft and can be turned.
But take your moody self, and walk away.

Ace of Spades

The others worked outside me. I,
tucked in myself, was trying to die.
I did not want to eat or drink
be stuck with IVs, walk (!) or think.
They'd try to talk, I'd only hear
Weird vocalizing, quacking, queer.
I turned away. I faced the wall.
I did not want the world at all.

And there he lay. My lovely Death.
So gently waiting. Breathed my breath.
I felt his own upon my face.
Such tenderness. Such loving grace.
If now's my time to go with you,
This time I can. It's okay, Boo.

'The Passionate Transitory': Poetry and Sincerity

VONA GROARKE

'A true note on a dead slack string' was how Patrick Kavanagh described poetry, but it all depends, I daresay, on what you mean by 'true'. Poetry has an uneasy relationship with sincerity: too much, we say the poem is navel-gazing; the poet, self-obsessed. We decide that we find nothing there relevant or helpful to the lives the rest of us are trying, hard, to negotiate. Too little, and we think the poem glossy and insubstantial, with not sufficient purchase in one life to tell the truth of life.

(There's often a performative element to sincerity: watch it watching itself from the wings, appraising its own authenticity, in parentheses.)

It's a delicate balancing act. As poets, we seldom want a poem to be relevant to only ourselves: we thrive on the possibility that if we make it well enough, a reader will be pleased to recognize herself in the poem we made of something in our lives. But we also know that trying too hard to appeal can knock a poem off balance, if it has no core.

(I'm generalising. I may have already lost your interest. That 'we' is so impersonal you may already have concluded I have no investment in this argument. And if I don't, why should you? Let me try, therefore, to rein it in.)

A certain kind of poem has a bourgeois dislike of the exposed emotion, throwing upon it layers of tea towels, jackets, tablecloths, blankets - whatever is to hand to cover it up, for heaven's sake; for decency. We know such poems: they come in familiar packaging – narrative poems (if they have historical subject-matter, then so much the better); anecdotes, puns, ballads about current affairs, ditties, song lyrics, 'comic verse'. There's a received quality to them, always; a formula down into which is dropped the kind of personal inflection that is, we know, really nothing of the sort.

(Oh yes, I'm being judgmental. These I call 'folk poems', tied up in the tight ribbons of locked-down quatrains and full rhyme with a customs declaration on the brown paper of their packaging: 'No dangerous substance here'.)

These kinds of poems get read out on the radio, occasionally, by jokey, likable hosts, but their natural habitat is probably the deaths column of local newspapers where they are paid for, by the word, in the hope that they honour the deceased and say something about the grief of the bereaved that needs to be said in something other than the language of everyday. Which may be why most memorial verses are written in rhyme. There's a formal neatness to it that might be said to dignify the occasion of a death; but also a way of squaring off the rawest feeling behind the four bars of a quatrain, and the turned lock of a full rhyme.

We will suspect, reading them, that there is feeling at the nub of them, sincere grief, but that feeling is muffled in borrowed form and ready-to-wear sentiment. The point of these verses is to be about grief, but not so much that we might think them actually written out of the feeling of grief at its most extreme. Form and language tame the feeling, like a bested dog. Instead is a simulacrum of feeling; a one-size-fits-all 'sincerity' without any personal investment and, therefore, without any risk.

(Why am I picking on these verses, that do no harm to anyone and maybe some good to a few?)

When it comes down to it, everyday language doesn't always seem equal to the task of conveying what's keenly felt or fiercely experienced: there's a gap, sometimes, (a chasm?) between experience and our wherewithal to describe it. Then we have two choices, really: firstly, tame the experience, dial it down or push it aside so either it doesn't need to be translated into language at all, or the language of everyday is adequate to the job of its conveyance. Alternatively, we can up our language game, find better words; braver, more passionate, sturdier, more elegant, more eye- and ear-catching words. What's needed, in that case, is a box of words put up on a high shelf and taken down only for special occasions. That's the box with the 'poem words', we might tell ourselves. And whenever life spills over the rim of the ordinary, we'll know exactly what to do. Up go the arms, down comes the box, in goes the hand, and out comes a fistful of only the most excellent words to be sifted down to the page, where they will settle into the likeness of a poem.

(The problem with a notional box is that it's never quite where you think you left it. I can reach now, for all I'm worth, and not put my hand to it.)

That fancy language does not make a poem is known to anyone who has tried to write one. Plain language neither, though its shorthand sometimes knows how to cover ground more efficiently. The task is to personalise our language, somehow, without sacrificing meaning to neology. We need to be original, yes, but not *too* original.
(In poetry, but in prose also, we push to discover and play with new form. It might not work but that's ok: the effort, the curiosity has value. Wouldn't you say?)

And we need to be sincere –or at least appear to be- without sacrificing style – more so in a poem than in life. In life we get away with all kinds of worn-down phrases, so long as we can accompany them with a true look in our eyes. Language is a two-way mirror and anyone saying 'I love you' likely cares not a whit for all the times it's been said before.

(Can you see, for the sake of it, the true look in my eye now?)

Sincerity, rightly deployed, can pierce the surface of a poem, as it can sometimes do the ordinary business of a life. We have come to expect it of poetry. I blame the strategic disclosures of the Confessionalist style but really it's a useful, tried and trusted trope whenever the lyric 'I' feels the weight of the poem's formal scaffolding, and threatens to buckle or warp. It could be that the artifice of poetic form dominates the voice; or it could be that the choices made for the poem begin to squeeze it into positions uncomfortable; or that the poem's voice begins to adopt a tone that has moved so far from the poet's own, that she begins to feel at sea. A remedial repositioning is deemed necessary. Out goes rhetoric; out goes the play of irony and the glitter of metaphor. The poem is reined in; the language toned down; the pyrotechnics of style held back while the trump card of, 'Oh, but look - it's *true'* is played as a winning move.

(If you can believe it. If you're prepared to.)

I'm inclined now to whittle sincerity down into three poetry strands of expression: grief and desire, of course, but also something less obvious and less pindown-able; something I think of as kicking in when the poet intensely engages with something outside herself, such that her inner self retunes to it and both inner and outer worlds are in perfect and enthusiastic equilibrium.

(Can equilibrium be enthusiastic? What should I call it: Epiphany? Too big. Connection? Too small. In-sync sincerity? Oh, come on now! Language fails me. This isn't good. Do I need to straighten my thinking, refine my argument?)

Grief, we expect to be sincere, at least to some extent. The expression of it may not be original, but we will believe it to be true in direct proportion to the simplicity of its expression. In the famous final stanza of Wordsworth's 'She Dwelt Among the Untrodden Ways', for example, the effect is deflationary:

She lived unknown, and few could know
When Lucy ceased to be;
But she is in her grave, and, oh,
The difference to me!

The quietness of the final phrase is a stylistic choice, of course, as is the slight shift in register from the first two lines of the quatrain to the understated, almost whispered, declaration of the second. It moves us, for a finish, because it strikes us as entirely sincere. Initially, we're unlikely to question how the effect of that sincerity has been wrought but if we keep re-reading the poem,

we're unlikely not to notice that it is an affect as delicately-wrought and finely-tuned as any successful poetic affect will be.

(But am I moved? Or just curious enough to want to remove the cover and look inside the machine of the thing?

The bathetic cadence of the final couplet is striking because of the contrast with the tone of the more self-consciously literary opening lines ('She dwelt among the untrodden ways / Beside the springs of Dove'), with their ballad metre and stylised language ('dwelt', for example, when 'lived' would have been perfectly adequate). The poem positions itself initially on a slightly higher rung of the Poetry Ladder than where it chooses to end, and that contrast between art and truth is what makes the final couplet so apparently sincere and so inherently affecting.

(Does it seem too disingenuous, I wonder, to position sincerity inside a frame of artifice?)

Come at from a different angle, the point of a poem might be to oppose or undermine that artifice, to strike straight for that true note, no matter how slack or taut the string. I'm thinking now of the glosses written by monks in the margins of ninth-century illuminated manuscripts, that are all (apparent) spontaneity and immediacy. Here's one (translated from Irish by Thomas Kinsella):

How lovely it is today!
The sunlight breaks and flickers
on the margins of my book.

It has the quality of something overheard. The scribe, tired of copying Latin grammar, perhaps, looks up from his desk in the scriptorium, notices the world outside, and jots his noticing down on the vellum that is his copybook.

(Which, of course, is how I write too. In my copybook.)

The scribe's task is not to be original, particularly – his work is copying. There is no place there for the personal, one would think. But that's not what happens: his noticing, his attention paid is like a stab in the arm, cutting through artifice and craft; personalising what is otherwise a gorgeous exercise in technical mastery. It's an outward glimpse that flicks to a glimpse of an inner world, being experienced immediately and through the senses, and with such urgency that it begs a record because it is at such moments of sheer sensation that we feel most human, and who amongst us cares to squander that feeling of intense vitality?

(I, for one, hoard them and dote on them, nightly, like Silas Marner with his gold coins.)

What cares the scribe if his jottings down will get him in trouble later for the cheek of them, set against the holy word? For him, it's a short line from feeling to the record of it; after all he is a scribe, so he inscribes his impulse on the expensive vellum, with the expensive ink. It is what he has to hand on which to put down what we all wish to put down, the fact that once, if only for a single and piercing moment, he felt himself, sensuously, to be very much alive.

(Which is the point of writing, surely? If not, then what is?)

Here, from across five centuries, is another such utterance, one I read as offering one of those rare moments when a reader can not only understand what's being said, but can actually *feel* the feeling of the poem.

O Western Wind, when wilt thou blow
    That the small rain down can rain?
Christ, that my love were in my arms
    And I in my bed again!

The words were written, set to music, in a 1530 partbook, but may be much older than that. It may be a fragment of a longer Middle English poem, the rest of which has gone the way of the scribe's unrecorded responses to what mattered less to him.

(I really hope not. Let it be complete in itself, perfect as it is.)

'O Western Wind' is by Anon. That helps. If we could fix a face and a build to its poet, I suspect it would seem less immediately forceful: we'd read it as his utterance, or hers. But in floating (almost) free of an historical physical frame, it seems to offer us a space in which to easily paste our own image. And it's only a very little jump from there to a full occupation of the poem, spoken in our own voice and representing our own longing, our own loneliness.

It's an ephemeral poem, in the sense that it articulates a single feeling, of a single moment, doing so in a way that impresses us with its ringing authenticity. I don't read these four lines and suspect the poet started off with the rhyming end words, with poetic strategy rather than sincere feeling, and simply took it from there.

(Does any poet believe a poem to have started once those formal decisions have been made?)

I don't read it thinking the poem has got in the way of that feeling, or has compromised or exaggerated it. What hits home here is the emotional content, and the mechanism of its conveyance – the quatrain's metre and b-b rhyme, its two punctuation marks (question and exclamation), the urgency of its monosyllabic thrust, its 'w' alliteration to push the poem off, the doubling of that 'rain' in line 2, the unusual adjective (which is also the only adjective in the poem, apart from 'Western', which is really part proper-noun – all seems secondary to the urgency and depth of feeling there. I notice these technical aspects of the poem, of course I do, but I perceive them to be only a kind of light scaffold to support the real business of the poem, which is its unadorned, undisguised sincerity.

(I've made the poem climb the scaffold of craft. There it is now, on the viewing platform, where I have already positioned myself to look it in the eye.)

Although music is provided in that 1530 version, I hope never to meet the poem that way: I don't want it mediated or accompanied. Leave it be, I say. Leave it pure and leave it stark: as such, it has already done what any poem may hope to do – it has made me both admire and feel. Head and heart, both implicated.

(Nothing like the knife-edge of desire to cut through to the quick of us!)

I first read the poem as a kind of promissory note on the poet's next encounter with her lover. It's a poem designed to be a charm to make that encounter happen; to make her desire come good.

Now I'm not so sure. The western wind is not a northern wind: its storms are of an altogether tamer variety. I realise now that the me reading those first two lines had been primed by poetry to expect every wind to be a gale, and every gale to be a tempest, and every tempest to be a metaphor for romantic intensity. I read the poem as if it were a second cousin, twice-removed, to Emily Dickinson's 'Wild nights, wild nights' or to Ted Hughes' 'This house has been far out at sea all night'. Put 'wind' and 'blow' in a line of poetry, and I was a reader to hear it immediately roar about my ears as if I were wandering out on the moors, haunted and bereft.

(But this essay is not about me.)

But that's not right, is it? The wind from the west is a clement wind: as winds go, it's inoffensive. The rain will be only small rain: no self-respecting bough would bother to bend for its desultory airs. You could uphold an umbrella in a west wind, no bother. You could even, were you so inclined, chance a tightrope walk.

What's asked for in the poem is not the wind to cause impassioned ructions in a scene of implacable calm. What's asked for is a wind to relieve not dullness, but heat. The setting is summer, parched and crinkly, not uproarious wintertime. Even small rain will be welcome: better than nothing, it will bring light relief. Or none. I don't believe the speaker is likely to lie with his or her lover anytime soon. The parched place may be, eventually, relieved by rain, but the other parchment, on which is written the anguish of loss, is harder to get to lie down.

(Oh, see me arranging my argument! I smooth, as rain might do, the jagged edge.)

By the time I encountered this poem I was old enough to recognise in drought a workmanlike metaphor for all kinds of lack, but especially of the sexual kind against which Patrick Kavanagh railed. The line that connects the first two lines with the second is a tripwire of sexual desire. It's not just a homely domesticity that's invoked, or the niceness of being comfortable in bed while a storm (of any kind) has its way with outside the house; it's not a *nice* poem in that way. It's a kind of howl of loneliness, of sexual frustration, that cuts through the intervening five centuries (at least) since its composition, to strike us with its naked sincerity.

But sincerity is not a sustainable condition: it does better with the puncturing instant than any longer time-frame. Even within the fourteen lines of a sonnet, it's possible to watch a poem slip in and out of an apparently fine-tuned honesty, like the dial on an old valve radio, sliding into signal and growing in volume as it warms to the voices its finds.

(Being also a way to live: silence brushing over voices, seeking itself out again.)

Patrick Kavanagh's poetic voice slips and slides this way. 'The Hospital', for example, kicks off with a stark avowal – he's telling a story in his first three lines, and he's colouring it in. In line three, the narrative impulse stalls: the poem shifts from narrative to descriptive register and the first false note of the poem is sounded in the phrase, 'an art lover's woe', a phrase with a whiff of the phony built-in, there to plump up the rhyme with, on the previous line, 'row'. The dial has slipped over a station, and it's a pity, because it was playing a good song.

Tricky, of course, to get every line shipshape in a Petrarchan sonnet, all the rhymes locked in, the argument argued, the register sustained. And interesting too, to watch a sonnet strain after the smoothing of so much. With Kavanagh's sonnets, a slack line often follows a taut one, as in lines five and six here:

But nothing whatever is by love debarred,
The common and banal her heat can know.

He very nearly had it, until that 'heat' which seems to me to be a 'poeticism', there to fill out the metre, there because in Kavanagh the strains of poet and Poet tend to be locked in constant duel. In this case, the signals of literal and figurative cross: he's used an abstract noun ('love'), and now he has either to climb back down from it, or to intensify. Unfortunately, he chooses the latter, diminishing a very powerful statement with an insincerity too far.

(Does anything sound less genuine than sincerity going a smidgen too far?)

He uses the Volta to recover, to find sure footing again in the material, real world. And it's lovely, the sestet: sure-footed placename and close observation opening out, unforced and elegant, to a final couplet that carries the whole weight of the poem as if it were lights as sticks.

In the best of Kavanagh, he nails it, just like that. 'Epic', for example, doesn't waver. The dial rests on the sweet spot it finds between Inniskeen, Munich and Ancient Greece. The proper nouns are a kind of ballast to holds the poem secure.

It's when he looks up into the stony grey sky that the problem sometimes occurs. That's when we see his language strain under the charge of having to be poetry.

(We know that strain; at least, I do. We buckle under it every time we want a phrase to turn a corner and find itself somewhere between the cul de sac of experience and the thoroughfare of style. Clumsy metaphor, I'm aware. I'm buckling, you might say.)

The sincere moment in a poem is exactly when we least feel the poet's acknowledged formal responsibility. The language seems charged only with urgency, and barely at all with considerations of poetry. 'Get it down quick', you can almost hear the monk say to himself. 'Get it down quick' says Anon too, but he has more time on his hands and no one breathing down his neck in the Scriptorium, so he has a little more leisure and headspace to apply poetry to urgency, and to craft impulse.

Wordsworth, our man in the scriptorium, Anon – they know the value of the 'passionate transitory'. They have found the compelling balance between their own experience and what might be thought of as our answering one. And they have applied just the right amount of poetry to confer on it a kind of completeness and self-containment that makes it memorable (in every sense of the word). Recorded without claptrap, in language that welds craft to experience, we feel the heat of their sincerity and we can't help but warm to it.

(If we do.)

The Hospital

A year ago I fell in love with the functional ward
Of a chest hospital: square cubicles in a row
Plain concrete, wash basins - an art lover's woe,
Not counting how the fellow in the next bed snored.
But nothing whatever is by love debarred,
The common and banal her heat can know.
The corridor led to a stairway and below
Was the inexhaustible adventure of a gravelled yard.

This is what love does to things: the Rialto Bridge,
The main gate that was bent by a heavy lorry,
The seat at the back of a shed that was a suntrap.
Naming these things is the love-act and its pledge;
For we must record love's mystery without claptrap,
Snatch out of time the passionate transitory.

Patrick Kavanagh

Two Poems

DAVID WHEATLEY

Alteration

i.m. Derek Mahon

Sunt aliquid manes. You'll know the line –
polite fiction the dead and living talk.
O clock-hands ticking out your time and mine,
the self-subtracting hours they gave and took:
words inch youwards but still want to know
which version of you they are talking to.

Come in from or accept again the cold.
I struck out for the nearest snow-fringed field,
following where a high, lone osprey called.
I tried to try your shadow on and failed.
My down, not feathers, was made less for flight
than an earthbound vertigo that's all my fault.

Your dandy's arcs and feints on high insist
there are places still the suave marauder
makes his cosy own. But Kinsale is lost:
the routed earl has crossed the silvered water,
the lone grey tidal breach that marks your passage
and no reflux can seal up or assuage.

The infinite changes and what stays the same
is that one point where options all run out.
I see the osprey, claws first, spin, take aim,
dive remorseless and first time get it right.
The trick is less to alter than dissolve
all forms now dead that do not salve or solve.

Chiaroscuro

A torch on his head the jogger in the park
swims up from the coalface of the dark.
Abroad before the bloodless winter sun
I scan the black for tears through which leak in
a street-sweeper's lemon high-viz glow,
late Christmas lights left on all night for show.
Yet dark is the element that holds me close,
still pregnant with the hedgerows' morning calls
below bare trees that keep guard as we sleep
and wait now to assume a daylit shape.
Not once but twice around the block careers
an early bus to rev up work-day cares
with every jolt for folk who're nae sae braw
after the fug of last night's last hurrah.
A tractor idles by the Co-op while
a dog is tethered by its monstrous wheel
but you remain where I left you swaddled tight
inside the duvet's latibule of night,
breath mingled in the chill with our twa bairns
while arse flap-slapped a vagrant cat returns.
And I in the dark am exposed to all that comes,
night fears at large till morning coffee calms.
So where am I bound but where a stove is lit
and the outline daylight draws draws up a seat.
The chiaroscuro of a half-drawn blind
leaves light and darkness made, remade, entwined
as day admits me like a watched-for omen,
the café door swung wide with a hoarse 'Come in'.

Dutch Supplement

in association with

Nederlands
letterenfonds
dutch foundation
for literature

The poets in this selection are a snapshot of the work set in motion by their translators. Unlike with the chronological deposition of our own literature, foreign poetries tend to be disclosed to us piecemeal, and selections often come to us in a temporal anomaly, whereby new generation poets such as Radna Fabias and Miek Zwamborn appear alongside established contemporary classics like K. Michel. Translators are usually key in this regard, and it is often their championing of a poet that leads to publication. But while poets such as Menno Wigman, Leonard Nolens, Toon Tellegen and Esther Jansma are already published in the UK, some of the major figures of Dutch poetry, such as Eva Gerlach and Gerrit Kouwenaar, have yet to be discovered.

The poets in this selection are writing within a recognisable European tradition, but possess a sensibility, insight and worldview that is subtly unfamiliar to us, whether they depict the Dutch urban experience, the relationship with the natural world, in Zwamborn's case her view of the Hebrides, or the colonial experience, with Fabias portraying the Dutch Antilles. What does unite these poets, though, is that, with the exception of Hester Knibbe (Eyewear), they are all yet to have collections published in the UK.

Erik Lindner and Radna Fabias will be published in North America this autumn, by Vehicule Press and Deep Vellum respectively.

Edited by P.C. Evans

Two Poems

K. MICHEL

Translated by David Colmer

Bookkeeping

my accountant comes to visit
together we clear a table
for his leaning tower of folders
my sister comes in
she acts very cranky towards him
first she's wearing a baggy tracksuit
the kind ballerinas wear when warming up
a little later an all denim outfit
what's up with the foul mood
I whisper in the hall
well I was just at the doctor's
and basically he said I'm going to die
what a nitwit I say

you've been dead for ages
and we burst out laughing
and then she goes to the dry cleaner's to pick up the
    curtains
while I write down this poem
in the living room, no idea
where the accountant's got to

every night lately it's the same thing
sometimes with a duffel bag sometimes in a floral
    dress
this way my books will never balance

Out of the Dark Sky

Out of the dark sky
snow whirls
shining softly
My sock absorbs the snow
through the hole in my shoe
Back in the green house
my sock leaves a snow print
on the red tiles
The tracks follow me
evaporating on the way
to the wide kitchen table

Where dear friend I am now
drawing up the report
– in all of nature
there is nothing that rolls up
except money given half a chance
everything slides downhill
– 'getting close to the bottom'
the bankers look over the edge
where Europe's silver has gone
– yes but what are they standing on
to peer into the abyss

– and is credit built
step by step on trust
– or is it a question
of constantly moving
goods ships harvests
databases downer cows bonds
moving them so quickly
the bottomlessness stays hidden

and while you and I promise to pay it all
back later later to me and him
the house trembles in the credit storm

of these snow-flurry days
and billions of zeroes tumble through the universe

– yes no yes let's put another log
on the fire and our heads together
because if we all concentrate the full
one hundred percent there is really
not a single problem we cannot ignore

what i hid

RADNA FABIAS

Translated by David Colmer

rims
the impeccably polished rims shining in the sun
   too big and too expensive for the cars they spin under

the tinted windows of the cars with the shining rims
the almost horizontal drivers of the cars with the tinted
windows and the shining rims
the explosive bass from the subwoofers installed in the
trunks
the dust from the dry fields
and pomade: green
or the black version

          smells of oil refinery
           perfect
for the hair of the modern *neger* in the 1980s
           perfect
to accentuate the natural blackness, to make it gleam
           perfect
for catching the dust
from the dry fields where spiky bushes grow
the dust
carried on the trade wind
         all around and all over
the poky bars
on the side of every road, blacktop or dirt
the women behind the barred windows of the bars on the
side of the road
the women
the holes
the women on the streets
        but not after dark
the holes in the road
the men
who drink beer beer beer at the bars on the side of the
road sometimes a whisky coke and

        finally
        find the car
        finally
        drive off
        finally
        find the house
        finally
        get home
        finally
find the woman who wasn't drinking at the bar on the
        side of the road
        finally
        search for her pussy
and recognize where they are from her pussy
        which house it is
        which of the many

women
with butts butts butts hoisted into leggings

booties like bumpers on which to hitch to an adjacent
island
        so they say
women who wear their clothes like a second skin
        no such thing as two sizes too small
men with greasy fingers under a makeshift carport next
to their house
bent over the engine of a car
sweating beer bottle in hand
        that carport's called a garage and
        that's a mechanic
        when he says shokkashobba
        he means shock absorbers
        shocks
they wear out so fast there
        because of the holes in the road past
men
with clippers and razors under a tree
        men like that are called barbers
men who come to collect money
        men like that are called arabs
men
under a tree with weapons and whisky
        men like that are called thugs
        irresistible
to women
with babes in arms
the smell of their burnt skin
in the sun
the golden sun
the gold teeth
women
whose hair will smell of chemical relaxer for days to
come
on top of that the burnt smell of their baked hair
        because it has to be smoother
        and it doesn't need to be hair
plastic
on the heads and fingers of women
women with curlers
the candy-colored houses
the churches
the churches painted the color of ripe bananas
the tamarind trees
the iguanas
the lizards with half-amputated tails
the free-range goats
the crowing roosters
the dogs chained to trees
the stray dogs that have been run over
the stray dogs asleep under cars that leak oil

the bullets that sound like fireworks

the fireworks to scare off evil spirits
the bullets to scare off evil people
the bullets fired by angry people
the newspapers full of blood
the heavy, throbbing motorcycles ridden by heavies
the old women on the side of the road
selling lottery tickets
selling hope
on the side of the road
by the holes in the road
in the dust
the street kids on undersized bikes
the way they dance their bikes around girls who have just
                    started menstruating
the mothers who warn about them
the mothers
                                                only
the dust
the lawn in the people who can afford a sprinkler's front
yard
                                            greener
the color of the people who can afford a sprinkler
                              lighter than
the junkie in the people who can afford a sprinkler's
front yard
the stuff under the junkie's arm in the people who can
afford a sprinkler's front yard
the deep black color of the street junkie with the thickly
callused feet
                            natural sandals
the wrecked cars
the litter
the thirsty earth
the apocalyptic downpours
the wind
the hurricanes
the telenovelas
        the silicone breasts of the women in the telenovelas
the bloody news from nearby countries
the beauty pageants
                    the silicone breasts of miss venezuela
the native language
the official language
the unofficial language
the unofficially segregated supermarkets
the unofficially segregated schools
the decapitated rooster in the woman across the road's
backyard
the woman across the road's tarot cards
the woman across the road's incense
the incense in the banana-yellow churches
the churches

the fortune tellers
the brujas who serve the gamblers
the gambling
                    tomorrow maybe win tomorrow maybe win
the sweating bodies rubbing up against each other
                                    that's called dancing
the heat
the washcloth in the bus driver's pocket
the fans blowing hot air
the processions of mournful people
the people who throw themselves on a loved one's coffin
and scream
                                    that's called mourning
the cemeteries where human remains are shelved one on
top of the other
the women's voices saying the rosary
the transistor radio
the women's voices on the transistor radio saying the
rosary
hail marys
our fathers
the raised voices of the people on the transistor radio
the dj talking through the songs on the transistor radio
the requests the dj talks right through on the transistor
radio
the sudden falling of the night
the justified fear in the night
the ghosts
the rippling blacktop
the lack of escape routes
the lack of seasons
the lack

the way everything is surrounded by sea
the way everything is scorched by the sun

the horror
the tourists
                            always smile at tourists
                            that's called manners
the sun
the blue
the impossible blue of the sky
the impossible blue of the sea
the fishermen in boats floating on the impossibly blue,
transparent sea
the sand
the washed-up fish tails on the white sand
the white sand against the impossible blue of the sea
the white sand that looks suspiciously like the dust
the dust

'Gloriously Filthy Tongues'

an interview with Dutch-Antillean poet Radna Fabias

MICHELE HUTCHISON

Radna Fabias (Curaçao, 1983) was born and raised in the Dutch Antilles and moved to the Netherlands at the age of seventeen. She studied Drama Writing at Utrecht's Academy for the Arts. Her debut collection *Habitus* (2018) won win six major awards, establishing her as one of the most striking new voices in Dutch poetry.

The collection's title is inspired by the work of French sociologist Pierre Bourdieu. His concept of *habitus* refers to the way individuals perceive the social world around them and react to it.

Michele Hutchison: What effect has winning these prizes had on your writing practice? Are you able to shut it all out?

Radna Fabias: What happened in the last two years is only really sinking in now. It was intense. My writing wasn't focussed on the public or on publication. Before my collection came out, I was writing away in peace and quiet. I remember discussions at the academy about when you can call yourself a writer – is it only when you have readers? I think you are a writer if you're writing, but they made valid points. I sent a poem to a poetry competition and it won a prize. Someone in the jury, a poet, sent it to her publisher without me knowing. Then the publisher got in touch and asked if I had more. I sent some poems, but not directly because the way I work is quite circumlocutory. I call it all writing but I was conducting interviews, collecting notes, films, pictures, audio clips, recording things that were important to me. Whenever I was in Curaçao visiting family I would take note of particular images and voices. I was writing and collecting everything that was meaningful to me.

I spent the last two years away from home a lot, giving readings and interviews. The way I'd structured my writing around my job was no longer sustainable. I know having an office job comes with its own special kind of suffering, I did it for a long time, but it did provide relentless structure.

I was also asked so many questions about the collection, I read so many interpretations of my work and heard the reactions of so many people to the work. I became very aware of readers. Of their voices. This was new. I'm slowly getting used to it all and finding ways to deal.

I try to shut it all out. Sometimes I succeed. Some voices are quite loud. Sometimes I listen to trap music and burn sage. Sometimes I write back and put it away. Anything to get them out. I don't want readers in my writing space.

How did studying script-writing influence your poetry?

My course was called Writing for Performance. I was writing screenplays and plays, but also some poetry and observational prose. In Curaçao, the theatre I knew was more about comedy – it leans towards stand-up and was quite offensive. Men dressing up as women and people laughing at that in sometimes painful ways. Theatre was a way of presenting social discomforts and tensions there. No frills. I didn't feel particularly at home in the Dutch theatre world, and maybe even less so in film. I just wanted to learn to write better. I would have liked to have gone to America to study creative writing but that was too expensive. Here, I could have done something more traditional like studying Dutch literature, or journalism, but I didn't. I don't see all these things as completely separate worlds though. What I learned at the academy was craft and my technique which is to go hunting for material, a multi-media gathering of bits and pieces. I then look for ways to tell as much as I can. It doesn't matter if I use poetic techniques or those taken from the theatre or film. Everything is on an equal footing, all the material, no one genre or discipline is better, only I render things into written language at some point. I was convinced I could combine all these things in a way that could convey my vision of the world, myself and others, using language.

I worked on the collection thematically, setting up themes and consciously repeating them, looking for a continuous whole. That was something I learned from scriptwriting. It's all about montage.

It resulted in a traditional book, are you going to produce works in other formats?

At first I didn't know the material was going to turn into poems. I thought, for example, that part of it could be an installation. I'd go through my material and pick out things that are suitable for film or poetry, though they never stay as separate as they seem in the first instance. But all the material I collect usually turns into text so it's probable that a book will be the final result.

So you're working on another poetry collection?

Well I'm working on prose, but then when I say prose, not as a kind of self-contained, closed thing. When I read, I feel at home in anything that transcends or mixes genres.

Let's talk about which writers have inspired you.

I'm not only inspired by reading as by all the material I gather. Not all of it is textual. I really like Dutch poet Bert Schierbeek who was part of the COBRA movement, and Dylan Thomas, Etheridge Knight, Frank O'Hara, Ginsberg... and among contemporary poets: Mustafa Stitou,

Jack Underwood and many more.

I'm inspired by all kinds of writers from Nabokov to bell hooks, from Simone de Beauvoir to Georges Perec. I should name other influences because it's not just books. I took a lot of inspiration from music – from hip-hop, musicians like Biggie Smalls, the Wu Tang Clan, Lil' Kim. And the gloriously filthy tongues of the people I grew up with in the Antilles. Gospel, the rhythms and repetitions of New Orleans bounce music and Trap, the No-Wave music scene from late 1970s New York – it was all ugly but also fiery. But also grunge bands. Let's see, *tambú*. Music of the Antilles which is made with drums and a thing called a *chapi*, a hoe. I like some Dominican music, *Perico ripiau*. The name itself is great. Ripped parrot. And the steady mellow rhythms of reggae, some of the violence of dancehall. Everything just cast onto one heap. I try to take everything that touches me to my work space.

I also recorded the people on the island and was fascinated by the way they interrupt each other. There's a communal fire to that, the way they interrupt and add to a conversation, building it in layers. I tried to convey what it was about the rhythm that touched me.

Can you give us an example?

The first poem in the collection, *what i hid*, is supposed to be a kind of panorama. It makes clear what you can expect, the kind of voices, it sketches something that is clearly multi-layered and determines the location for that section. For a long time, I avoided the voices from where I came from and pushed them away so I didn't have to explain them.

But now you don't explain them, you place them in context.

Yes, the collection is really a composition of a lot of documentary material and I structured some of it like I would a documentary. I don't know how satisfied I will remain with the collection as my work progresses but I am very satisfied with the technique and methods.

For me it was like going on a journey to the place.

Exactly. A place with many layers. I was interested in a wide range of themes and many of them come together in the first poem. Even if you've never been to Curaçao I wanted to show some of it through the images and the way the images are put together and what my associations with the place are. I wanted the reader to feel like they had put on Virtual Reality glasses.

I think you really succeeded in that and that's why the book was so well-received.

I know some of my readers have been to the Antilles, but I was particularly interested in what people who haven't been take away from it. I heard from lots of people that they did get it, which was reassuring. I mean you can want these things, but will it work?
I've brought along a list of all the things I looked into when I was looking for a way of addressing the subject:

The suggestive power of montage.
Contradictions.
Collisions.
The Aristotelian definition of a tragedy.
Queneau's *Exercices de Style*.
Ways of presenting synchronicity.

I collected an entire document full of imperatives relating to women. You know how they always get told: *Do this, do that,* etc. But there are a lot of contradictions if you compare theoretical feminism with my own observations in the Antilles and the way women relate to each other there. The way women educate each other; the way the environment forms them.

What else? The magical dimension of language – as a way of summoning new energy. And going back to everything in relation to the mysticism that was dominant in my childhood. Magic versus Christianity.

I read about the way egos all interact with each other and how impossible it is to place the self outside of the social system. I remember reading about Schierbeek's dispersed perspectives and the multiple 'I's in relation to Elias' interaction model. And Bourdieu rocked my world. And after all that reading and form experimentation, I started looking into the rituals I grew up with.

Sounds like a lot more than you could fit in just one book!

I wasn't working towards a book. That's the point of working this way. It's all a larger project, constant research and collecting and writing. You don't produce for one book but sometimes you pause and distil something out of it.

When I was editor of Poetry International Web I noticed a certain public appreciation for poetry that is consciously political. Some people think poetry should be political. You don't, I think?

Poetry doesn't have to be anything at all. Not everyone has a choice, though. Sometimes a person's mere presence is political.

When people write close to their own experiences and their presence in the world is a political matter. I recently met a female poet from Palestine. She didn't intend to write political poetry. It became political due to the reader's appreciation of it. I think in this collection I have remained very close to my body, I have written from this specific body and its environment. I spoke to many other women, so they're present in my work. And a lot of our stories were similar, sadly. But was I planning to make a statement? No. I was preoccupied with language, with repetition, with being present in the world. That can be interpreted as political.

But then everything's political, life is political.

Right. Still, expectations based only on my appearance are exhausting. It's often no longer about what I write but about what is expected. Just because I thematise certain things doesn't mean I'm defending certain points of view. I'm not an activist. My poetry is too polyphonic and it's not transparent enough. I'm interested in everything that's *not* clear cut, the grey areas where ugliness overlaps with beauty. Not the moral line. I don't try to condone or condemn things. You need a certain dogmatic assertiveness to call people to action. There's not much in my poetry you could use as a slogan. I hope there's nothing in there you can march for without doubting or incriminating yourself.

What are your thoughts on translation and your experience of being translated? And I know you've worked with various translators into English.

It's a strange experience but when it works it's a minor miracle. When it goes wrong and the miscommunication is magnified it can be quite painful.

Because your work is very personal?

Yes, for example in relation to the first section in the collection which isn't set here. It was sometimes alienating to explain myself, particularly when it had to do with the translator having a different geographical and socio-economic background.

Also: sometimes translators are tempted to tone down the linguistic play otherwise it doesn't sound grammat-ically correct. They can have the tendency to normalise. But their standard is not necessarily mine. Some things are not trying to be correct. Some things are there with rhythm in mind, or are otherwise specific to my perspective.

Daniel Cunin's French translation of Habitus *captures the rhythm very well.*

We discussed things line by line. Sometimes in French we had to specify a gender while it could remain unspecified in Dutch. We had to look at *what* you give away *when* in the text. Do we already have to say this is a woman? I can also be a bit of a pain in the ass because some words summon up certain associations in me and then I'd rather have something else in the translation. Mainly I think it's important to have enough time to consult with the translator. But I have confidence in the result because I know how much close attention to language most translators pay, there's something of a poet in them too. I want my energy to come across and the feeling I get with certain words. I want translators to find something that evokes the same emotions in me and still works rhythmically. When they do there seems to be hope for mankind – perhaps we can understand another after all.

Two Poems

ROELOF TEN NAPEL

Translated by Judith Wilkinson

psalm *(lazarus)*

they tell you a friend is going to die. they know
you can help, they've seen your hands,
what they brought forth.

on purpose you leave too late, this body
must make a point. you arrive at the grave
and though you knew what was to come, and what will
    come,

you weep.
get to know us.

even what heals hurts, even what rises from the dead

is missed, we know by now that something always
stays behind.

the problem is that you are good, and we aren't,
that you arranged it that way. we are
a fish put in a puddle –

it's a cruel man, surely,
who stands beside it

shouting:
breathe now, rise up, just breathe.

song of songs

i am my beloved's and my beloved
is mine – he appears like the twilight,
his arms like the burning horizon,
his eyes like ravens, sheltering in the evening –

his lips are of copper, gleaming – oh
so moist – let him grab me with the grip
of his hands, taste me with his tongue –

let him quench my gehenna head –
my friend is blackened like the bridges of prague,
i want to wear down his baroque body with my fingers
and scratch him open like an old wound –

i give him my valley of the dead, the rancour
my heart still burns with – that he may know me
and kiss me with the kisses of his mouth

Two Poems

ESTER NAOMI PERQUIN

Translated by David Colmer

Due to Logistical Problems

On Wednesday we received a box
containing our future.

It was a mistake, of course, we realised that immediately.
On the phone the manufacturer was frantic.

Don't open it, whatever you do, don't open it. Someone
is on their way right now to pick it up.

We waited. Meanwhile we put the box in the middle of the room
on the rug. It was a big box. And heavy.
We drew conclusions, drank tea.

Then we took turns to press an ear against the cardboard. We made
out music, very soft music. The sound of cranes flying high
overhead. Hustle and bustle. A steam train,
clearly a steam train leaving the station.

When the bell rang we had just cut the packing tape.
Light was seeping out like liquid from a wound.
"I'm here for the box," someone yelled
through the slot. "Open up."

But we stepped cautiously into the box and saw that,
more beautifully than ever, we would forget
what we thought was in store for us.

Housekeeping

Returning from a wander past the city's foreign markets,
where they sell plucked ducks and live monkeys
under a waft of cinnamon and honey,
I found my hotel room as follows:

The bed had been made, the sand-coloured pillows fluffed,
the towels replaced, the floor vacuumed, the windows
cleaned, the ceiling whitewashed, the roses
in the wallpaper (large buds, short stems) had been watered,
my husband phoned to hear the word sorry, sorry, sorry, sorry

my dresses were more elegant, my boots svelte, the poem
I had started the night before lay finished
on the glass table next to the bed

and in a hand I had never seen before the words had been found
for the nameless emptiness I was always too scared to inhabit,
which I skirted with jokes, like someone who thinks
they've seen their own resting-place.

It was better than anything I could ever write, it broke
with every memory. On checking out I left a tip of
(at current exchange rates) one adult human life
and two days' despair.

Two Poems

MIEK ZWAMBORN

Translated by Michele Hutchison

Callinago callinago - Common snipe

In the marshy field wading birds stitch grass
to the earth's underlay

one of the birds ratchets itself up
a fan of quills vibrating in the air
the sound of thrumming feathers

rustling through withered tussocks of sedge
swiftly escaping a rasping beak
both of her wings pointing upwards like arrows
a salvo of pecks launched from simple clefts
the nest already open in the quaking bog

the second snipe ratchets itself up
wing-strokes parallel and rising
the response comes on four wings

heads catching the breeze in bursts
eyebrow stripes raised
before impregnating one another

brooders exist
egg-cosies and egg-timers exist
egg-racks and decorated eggs exist
square eggs exist
eggshell porcelain dishes exist.

Uria aalge – Guillemot

scant is the difference between rock and bird
feathers as black as the seaweed she settled on
her breast a white square now she is sitting

the hard afternoon sun sets her shadows upright
an angular guillemot glides along too

she laid her egg at the tideline
copying the oystercatcher

I think about this and remember a herring
hiding in a school of mackerel

how to understand animals
that break the rules or do I
break them myself by knowing what I do?

further along, redemption flies low over the water
Guillemots brood standing on rock ledges without
    nests
their eggs roll around and back between their feet

remember where they are and flip over the year
the birds' paint guns shooting
speckles and curls
on a fixed date an egg tooth taps open the shell

Can I be guessed? Or can I be known

HESTER KNIBBE

Translated by Vivien D. Glas

Can I be guessed? Or can I be known, broken down into
more than hair and skin, the sharpness of tooth and nail?

A bird flies through the air, wings so wide that you
can count its outstretched feathers, but who decodes its call?

Someone dancing nude in ballet shoes, arms spread,
may still be hiding their soul behind a tiny tattoo. I have

rooms with curtains drawn and nothing to conceal,
attics and cellars with locks and codes I routinely

reveal by blushing out of the blue. At times
I crack my hanker like a walnut, show

the halves in open hands: see this I. And only I
know the inimitable tumbling in my head.

I am a suburb

MARIA BARNAS

Translated by Donald Gardner

I Am a Suburb

Stood by the bus stop with a felt pen/ In this suburban hell/ And in the distance a police car/ To break the suburban spell/ Let's take a ride, and run with the dogs tonight/ In Suburbia/ You can't hide, run with the dogs tonight/ In Suburbia

Pet Shop Boys, 1986

Only the dogs run here and pant
to get to the edge of the suburb
that dissolves when you think you're close

they almost caught me in passing
yes I know the tale of the horizon.
It comes from the shrubs where Kim sits

and smokes or from behind the bus shelter
where the assailant loiters. Or from Ivan's
cellar he lets no one enter.

We don't know for sure if he exists.
With a bucket on his head he's a stupefied
superhero. What does he see that makes him pitch

like a ship in a stormy painting?
The dogs run to string all the suburbs

together to make a single city. And they go on
running for the sake of the blood that keeps on
 pulsing
and recalls a heart that clots.
And because nobody else does it.

Maybe one day they'll bring the heart back home
like an egg on the tongue entire and warm.
Hounds can do that: retain a jewel

of outer space. I make a list
of cheap flight destinations
the priciest first. I try another list

of places I'd most like to go. But where
should I begin? In the heart that is missing
I am fine. I am a suburb.

Two Poems

ERIK LINDNER

Translated by Francis R. Jones

from Tokens of identity

1. All that matters is for things to make a sort of sense,
the chance to be part of a whole, belong to a group,
a collective. People getting changed between
the low hedges by the barbed
wire round the dunes.

Playing-cards drop on an outspread towel, the picnic
under cloth in a wicker basket, sand heaped
over a bottle from the distillery where
one of us has worked that day. Like
everyone else we run to the sea

and back again, tap sand out of our shoes on the path,
embracing the unspoken in every conversation
when we say goodbye and feeling empty

in a tram as the driver announces
the stops to his only passenger.

from Ostende

2. The sea's the same size as the wind
it flows across the corestone
worked by the wind for the sea

a sandpiper runs along the wind
and counts with its steps

the free patches of sand
and the crests of sea blowing free
and the clumps of wind tumbling free

rolling creeping sliding fragments
of an island that briefly stands still
by the edge of the sea

hooves pound down the stone
the sea carries the bone ashore
the sand cools in the wind

clumps of foam mark out the size
of an island emerging for a little while
under a sandpiper's footsteps

beyond the wind above the sea.

The French spelling of the poem's title ('Ostend' in English) alludes to Henri Storck's silent film 'Images d'Ostende' (1929).

The detour via History – on Zbigniew Herbert

K. MICHEL

Translated by Donald Gardner

And so the intractable word 'thus': In the morning, five men are escorted across the yard and forced to stand against a blank wall. Five men, two of them young and the others middle-aged. Nothing more is known of them. Everyone holds their breath as the platoon level their rifles; all at once everything is blazingly clear in the garish light. The yellow wall, the cold blue sky behind the barbed wire instead of a horizon above the wall.

A poem from the early 1950s by Zbigniew Herbert begins with this description. It is not clear whether it refers to the German occupation or to the Stalinist terror and this is not important; it could be a description of any execution. Whatever the case may be, at the moment when the rifles are aimed, a revolt breaks out among the five senses that would gladly escape like rats from a sinking ship. But by then the bodies have already been floored and lie there covered up to their eyes in shadows. The poet goes on to write: I did not learn this today; I knew it before yesterday; so why have I written insignificant verses about flowers? And he asks what the men talked about in the night before their execution. About prophetic dreams maybe? About adventures in the brothel; a voyage; car parts; that vodka is the best beverage by far and that you can get a headache from wine; about girls, or fruit or about life.

By describing the last hours of these five men, the poet does justice to their memory, but he also brings a moral problem upon himself, namely what he can write about next in light of such a dramatic event. It is a question of such gravity that the poet does not seem able to offer any more answer than a diffident stammering, a flaming indictment or a pious silence. Herbert's response follows in the closing stanza, which begins with the word 'thus'; a 'thus' that originates in the illogical, and which claims the right of poetry to be poetry, precisely in light of atrocities, a 'thus' that affirms the capricious vitality of life and defies the power of death to tie one's tongue:

thus one can use in poetry
names of Greek shepherds
one can attempt to catch the color of morning sky
write of love
and also
once again
in dead earnest
offer to the betrayed world
a rose
(from 'Five Men'. Translated by Czesław Miłosz & Peter Dale Scott)

Herbert wrote the poem that I have described here when he was still young; however, he had already had personal experience of the emotional and moral drama with which the poem is imbued. He was born in 1924 in Lvov in a family that saw itself as Polish but which was really of a mixed background. On his mother's side there was an Armenian grandmother and on that of his father, an English great-grandfather. At the time, Lvov was a city in which a variety of ethnic groups lived together with Jews forming a considerable presence. When Herbert was fifteen, the city was annexed by the Russians and two years later this was followed by the German occupation. In the meantime, he took part in underground activities and studied at a clandestine university. After the city fell into the hands of the Russians in 1944, he moved to Krakow and then to Warsaw, where he studied economics, law and philosophy. In the years after the war, he started publishing poems but he turned his back on the official literary world once the pressure to write in the social-realist style had become too great. In 1951, he resigned from the Writers Union, an action that meant him being branded a non-person. In the following years, he earned his living as a bank clerk, a shop assistant, a designer of work clothing for the peat industry and an office manager of the Association for Polish Composers. He spoke of the suffocating isolation of those years in an interview published in *Die Zeit* on 8 August 1986. It is hard for us to imagine today, knowing the course that history took, how utterly without prospects he must have felt his position was. There were no signs to suggest that any alleviation of the political and cultural climate would occur; it was a realistic scenario that he would continue for dozens of years to exist as a 'nobody' and that he would write for no end other than to fill the drawer of his desk until his death. In this period, he developed a philosophical position that you could best describe as 'Stoic' and he adopted an attitude with regard to writing that was distinguished by a hard-boiled self-assurance, averse to any compromises with literary trends and mores. Fortunately, the climate thawed sufficiently after the death of Stalin for him to publish his first collection, *Chord of Light*, in 1956; two years later, in 1958, he was also able to travel extensively in Western Europe. After this first collection, he published a dozen books of poetry and three collections of essays; he also undertook many more journeys; he has spent long periods in Paris and Berlin and taught in America prior to his death in 1998.

It should be clear that due to the war and the successive waves of Russian and German occupiers, Herbert had built up an unforgettable experience of the caprices of history. And it should also be clear that due to the post-war power struggle with its accompanying ideological rhetoric, he acquired an idea of the way that words could be manipulated and how gruesome the consequences could be. The lessons he drew from his experiences as a poet led him to write in an unvarnished style, free of all rhetorical sensationalism, and to situate the events of his time in a much broader historical framework. He refused to be seduced by bitterness into writing angry indictments parading his moral rightness, nor did he fall into the trap of the anecdotal that clings to every

personal tragedy. Instead he wrote poems in a style that is permeated with wry humour and that provoke thought instead of preaching. Poems like 'From Mythology', which often took the form of historical parables.

'First there was a god of night and tempest, a black idol without eyes, before whom they leaped, naked and smeared with blood. Later on, in the times of the republic, there were many gods with wives, children, creaking beds, and harmlessly exploding thunderbolts. At the end only superstitious neurotics carried in their pockets little statues of salt, representing the god of irony. There was no greater god at that time.

Then came the barbarians. They too valued highly the little god of irony. They would crush it under their heels and add it to their dishes.'
(Translated by Czesław Miłosz & Peter Dale Scott)

From the first collection onwards, historical figures appear in Herbert's work. They come predominantly from Greek mythology or ancient history, but Spinoza and even Isadora Duncan make an appearance. Usually, he draws an incisive portrait, for instance of Prometheus grown old, who is sitting and writing his memoirs while in the kitchen his wife is bustling. 'The fire is crackling cheerfully in the hearth. On the wall there is a stuffed eagle and a letter of gratitude from a tyrant of the Caucasus, who succeeded in burning a rebel city thanks to Prometheus's invention. Prometheus chuckles to himself. This is now his only way of expressing his quarrel with the world.' Sometimes Herbert has the top people speaking; in this case they address us from the realm of the dead, for instance the Emperor Claudius who defends himself against accusations of cruelty (in reality I was only absent minded). Almost invariably Herbert gives us a totally new version of the life story or myth. He does so in the tone of someone unmasking the official interpretation of the facts and revealing the true circumstances. The Minotaur for instance in his version is no monster but a mentally-challenged prince with water on the brain. The labyrinth was built in order to teach him to think, a system of passages with different levels and stages of abstraction, an educational puzzle. The prince understands nothing of it and fails to develop his understanding. The king then decides to rid himself of this stain and orders the professional murderer Theseus to come 'from Greece, a land that was famous for its experts'. 'And Theseus killed the Minotaur. At this point, myth and history are in agreement. Theseus emerged from the labyrinth, the primer that had become irrelevant, carrying the huge bloody head of the Minotaur, with its goggling eyes in which for the first time something of the wisdom that is normally the fruit of experience had begun to sprout.'

'I like working with mythological material', Herbert said in an interview. 'Myths are primal images that the past would have us adopt as eternal truths, but which are often unfortunately revealed to be prejudices. [...] When I revert in my work to themes and myths from antiquity I don't do so out of coquetry – I am not interested in clichés or intellectual ornament – I try and knock on the ancient ideas of humanity to ascertain whether they sound hollow and if so, where. What is more, I search for an answer to the question of what meaning the once hallowed concepts of freedom and human dignity may still possess. I believe that their great binding content has not dissolved.' Herbert studied the past to gain an understanding of contemporary events and nothing is too old for him, as his German translator wrote, 'to provide a rich comparison to explain present-day occurrences.' Herbert rarely juxtaposed past and present; rather he saw the past as a component part of the present. The historical characters also bear a striking resemblance to contemporaries and he almost never uses them as allegorical instruments. They are no metaphors, but individuals with their own biography and psychology. It is as if figures from antiquity exist in the same temporal dimension as we do; as though one could speak of a single great historical continuum. How you might understand this can perhaps be elucidated by means of his poem 'Sequoia'. In it he describes a visit to a nature reserve in which these enormous trees are the main attraction. Somewhere in the park he sees a cross-section exhibited of a centuries-old tree trunk. In the pattern of the rings, someone has marked the sequence of historical events: 'an inch from the center the fire of Nero's distant Rome, and finally close to the bark's shoreline, the Normandy landings.' As the rings in the space of the Sequoia trunk exist alongside each other, so in Herbert's poetry the Rome of Claudius and post-war Poland share the same historical space. In a poetry festival in Klodzko in April 1972, where the theme was 'the poet and the present time', he proposed speaking about 'poetry and reality' because the space in which a poet works is not the time in which he lives but reality, that has a much more panoramic dimension.' The fact that Herbert locates events in a broad historical framework, does not mean that he has an essentialist vision of history or humanity; 'that is how it always is' or 'that's just human nature' – these are not ideas that you come across in his poetry. He usually writes about concrete individuals and specific events. He uses the historical perspective not to generalize, but to intensify.

The question however is justified as to what this detour via history precisely results in. Let us therefore look at an excerpt of a poem that appeared in his collection *Report from a Besieged City*. The speaker in the poem is Damastes, who has been categorized as a common brigand since antiquity. He only still enjoys any renown in connection with his nickname and his horrendous use of torture; he was the inventor of the 'Procrustes bed', an expression you often hear today in times of governmental formations and company takeovers.

from 'Damastes (Also Known as Procrustes) speaks'

in reality I was a scholar and social reformer
my real passion was anthropometry

I invented a bed with the measurements of a perfect man
I compared the travelers I caught with this bed
it was hard to avoid – I admit – stretching limbs
cutting legs

the patients died but the more there were who perished
the more I was certain my research was right
the goal was noble progress demands victims

I longed to abolish the difference between the high and the low
I wanted to give a single form to disgustingly varied humanity
I never stopped in my efforts to make people equal...

...I have the well-grounded hope others will continue my labor
and bring the task so boldly begun to its end
(Translated by John and Bogdana Carpenter)

In this poem, Herbert again turns a traditional tale upside-down. He plays the devil's advocate by giving Damastes the opportunity to exculpate himself. No, he wasn't a bandit; he was an inventor, a man with a noble vision of the future, a reformer who aimed to abolish the difference between high and low.

This voice of a figure from Greek antiquity sounds uncomfortably familiar. Who is there who does not remember the appeal to the new humanity and the merciless credo of progress? The closing lines, in which Damastes addresses the future, work like two pebbles that he casts into a well out of which a horrifyingly deep splash reverberates twenty centuries later.

In a meeting with the poet, his English translators, Bogdana and John Carpenter discussed this poem. When they pointed out that Damastes used certain modern expressions, he admitted that there was a certain parallel with Lenin. But they forgot to ask why he didn't simply use Lenin's name and why he didn't situate the poem in the present age; they only asked that later on. According to them, the most obvious answer, that censorship would make it impossible to publish a critical or ironic poem about Lenin, was the least important; in Herbert's work, the use of characters from antiquity and myths is seldom a pretext for avoiding censorship. The use of Lenin's name would have rid the poem of the constant interplay between past and present that it has now. It was precisely through not making any explicit reference to our time, by offering no commentary, and by employing as speaker a specific character from antiquity who tells a limited and concrete tale, that the poem gains that metaphorical power that enables it to embrace everyone who has been involved in cruel experiments like this with Utopian aims.

And in the midst of the uprisings, the pitched battles, the political grovelling, the objects of everyday use are always present – the chairs, the suitcases, the stones; and, stoically, they endure all that pressure. They are the unmoving counterparts of the human beings in the historic drama. This is why Herbert feels a particular affection for them. 'If not personally, certainly as a witness, I have experienced a number of times the collapse of ideologies, the dismantling of artificially created visions of reality, the humiliation of beliefs in the face of facts. And the realm of things seemed then to be a support, a point of departure that could lead to creating a vision of the world that corresponded with our experience. After the false prophets had departed, the things, so to speak, showed their innocent faces, untainted by the lies.' And in another interview he said that he was fascinated by objects, 'because they are so different from us, and so mysterious. They come from a world that is entirely different from ours. We never know for sure if we understand them; sometimes we think we do, sometimes not – it depends on the degree we project ourselves into them. What appeals to me is their ability to resist us, to be silent. We can never really conquer or tame them, and that is a good thing.'

The Pebble

The pebble
is a perfect creature

equal to itself
mindful of its limits

filled exactly
with a pebbly meaning

with a scent which does not remind one of anything
does not frighten anything away does not arouse
desire

its ardour and coldness
are just and full of dignity

I feel a heavy remorse
when I hold it in my hand
and its noble body
is permeated by a false warmth

 – Pebbles cannot be tamed
to the end they will look at us
with a calm and very clear eye

(Translated by Czesław Miłosz & Peter Dale Scott)

You could say that the pebble's gaze resembles that with which Herbert views the world, with this difference that in Herbert's gaze, no matter how sharp and unremitting it is, there is always an element of compassion. In the collection *Report from a Besieged City*, for instance, there is a poem about Maria Rasputin, a daughter of the notorious monk. Her father played a part in the drama around the last Tsar, but her role is far more modest; she was just one of a million extras. She left for America and worked as a housemaid for White Russian emigrants. She achieved fame in the circus with 'the Dance with the Bear', but an over-ardent embrace put a stop to her career. She proudly turned down an offer for her autobiography to be published under the title of *The Daughter of Lucifer*. 'She showed more tact', Herbert wrote, 'than a certain Svetlana' – Stalin's daughter. She was buried in America, 'unmourned by church bells, a priestly bass in a completely unsuitable place reminiscent of a picnic.' The poem is a sharp portrait of a drab and cramped existence, and also an ode to one of history's extras. Just for a moment Herbert rescues her from anonymity and commemorates her: 'Maria distant chatelaine / with your plump red hands // no one's Laura'.

In an essay that he wrote on the subject of his poem, 'Why the Classics', Herbert says that the dialogue with the past doesn't need to mean any flight from the present, any reaction out of disappointment; because undertaking a journey through time, with the baggage of all our experiences, to investigate myths and symbols, is an undertaking with great relevance for the present. And he concludes his essay with the following passage: 'One's awareness of the frailty and triviality of human life is less depressing if we set it in the chain of history, that is nothing other than the handing down of a belief in our deeds and our efforts. In this way, even the scream of horror can be transformed into a cry of hope.'

Reviews

The Wordsmith Taliesin

The Gododdin: Lament for the Fallen, a version by Gillian Clarke (Faber) £14.99
Reviewed by Gwyneth Lewis

At the end of the sixth century, the area in which Welsh was spoken reached as far north as Edinburgh. The names of five early Welsh poets are mentioned in chronicles. No work by Talhaearn Tad Awen ('Father of inspiration'), Blwchfardd nor Cian Guenith Guaut ('Cian, Wheat-Harvest of Song') survives but we do have manuscript copies of poetry by Aneirin and Taliesin. Both wrote in the service of war lords engaged in power struggles with their Celtic rivals and also Saxons pushing up towards Northumbria and west to the Welsh Marches. Both write vividly about the spoils of war and the horror of defeat. Taliesin left twelve short poems, mainly dedicated to his patron Urien Rheged, praising his flourishing kingdom. The only work by Aneirin we have is *Y Gododdin*, a body of roughly a hundred and fifty verses which were preserved in *The Book of Aneirin*, a thirteenth-century manuscript. The poem is in two versions, notated by different scribes. Linguistically, the work is Welsh but is claimed, geographically, as the first Scottish poem, by Robert Crawford in his *Penguin Book of Scottish Poetry* and in Thomas Owen Clancy's *The Triumph Tree: Scotland's Earliest Poetry AD 550–1350* (Canongate, Edinburgh, 1998).

During *Y Gododdin*'s passage from an oral performance poem to an early medieval manuscript text, Aneirin and Taliesin were considered contemporaries. In one section of *Y Gododdin*, Aneirin appears to have been taken captive:

I stretch out my knee in my earth house,
an iron chain about my knees.

For mead in the drinking horn,
for the men of Catraeth,
I, yet not I, Aneririn
the wordsmith Taliesin knows it –
sang *Y Gododdin*
before the new day dawned. (85)

To me, 'I, yet not I, Aneirin' is one of the most intriguing lines in early Welsh poetry, because it suggests that a poet, in their work, is both a self and unknowable. Aneirin describes himself as coming back bloodstained from battle, its only survivor. He's infected by death, in that the soldiers he praises can't hear him. The 'I, yet not I' phrase is even more apposite to Taliesin's corpus, collected together in *Llyvyr Taliesin*, ('The Book of Taliesin'). There the early poet of the Heroic Age is, in poems written by medieval poets and ascribed to him, mythologized into a shamanic shape-shifter. Textually, as well as imaginatively, then, he's a time-traveller. The Taliesin persona becomes a collective voice, an 'I' that is really 'we'. There is enough of an 'I' in Aneirin's work, though, to make the omission of his name on the title page curious.

In her version of Y *Gododdin*, Gillian Clarke joins her voice to her forebearer's; she both 'is' and 'is not' Aneirin; or, following T.S. Eliot, one could equally say that Aneirin is and is not Gillian Clarke. The 'Singer's Prologue', in which Clarke deftly weaves together lines from the A and B texts, sets the tone in her own highly assured and lyrical account of the poem:

Gododdin, I sing your epitaph,
in the hall before the hearth,

here before the gathered throng
where our soldier-poet sang....

When earth covered him, Aneirin,
poetry departed from Gododdin. (3)

Clarke's *Gododdin* looks deceptively like a successor to Alice Oswald's *Memorial*, which was subtitled *An Excavation*. Clarke notes that '*Y Gododdin* is archaeology in the form of song' (viii) but, whereas *Memorial* is a selection of individual elegies lifted out of the epic action of *The Iliad*, *Y Gododdin* is a complete text combining recitative and aria, needing no excision. Both are oral poems before being transcribed and both strike a similar tone of grief for slaughtered young men.

Y Gododdin is named after the tribe which goes to fight what turns out to be a catastrophic defeat in Catraeth, or Catterick, in around the last decade of the sixth century. In school, we memorized the most famous verse of the cycle, which gives the plot précis:

Gwyr a aeth Gatraeth, oedd ffraeth eu llu,
Glasfedd eu hancwyn a gwenwyn fu,
Trychant trwy beiriant yn catáu,
A gwedi elwch tawelwch fu.
Cyd elwynt lannau i benydu,
Dadl ddiau angau i eu treiddu.

Clarke's keen ear for music allows her to weave rhymes into English that are equivalent but excitingly different from the Welsh pattern, conveying the sound admirably:

Men rode to Catraeth, debonair,
Their snare, the honey-trap, gold mead.

Three hundred men called up to war –
and after joy, the hush of death.

Though they went to church for pardon
just three survived, for their sins.

In the second line of the poem, the mead is usually translated as 'poisonous' to the soldiers. Clarke, a beekeeper herself, chooses to foreground mead as a 'honey-trap'. This leads to gains and losses. In previous sections Clarke has translated 'caeog' – 'torque' – imagined as a 'snare of the enemy' as 'the correct but less effective 'brooch'. She's keeping her metaphorical powder dry for the mead, which she sees as a golden loop in a cup, a stunning and original image. While I think that 'honey-trap' is daring but works colloquially and as an image, I feel that 'for their sins' in the lines above doesn't catch the theological seriousness of the Welsh, which is more like:

Though they went to church to repent
Death's implacable logic ran them through.

Translating early Welsh poetry is an extreme sport, requiring match fitness. I find tracing Clarke's reasons for her choices fascinating, because it gives an insight into her imagination as she performs these elegies. In the end, my quibbles are a matter of taste. For example, in the elegy for Cibno, for example:

He hand-fed the crows...
He wore gold
in the front row
in the war of heroes. (177)

'Adar' in the original refers to birds in general and could be portraying a man, in peace time, holding grain for pets. Clarke's specifying crows here is confusing, given that eagles, ravens and wolves gorge on the carcases of the defeated army. In the poem immediately preceding, 'Gwawrddur', the soldier is described as feeding 'ravens on the fortress wall', a line which I'd read as the hero being food for scavengers. Gododdin's soldiers feasted before the battle, animals feast on the fallen men. Then again, these are choices which Clarke-as-Aneirin is entitled to make.

If *Llyvyr Taliesin* is *The Odyssey*, then *Y Gododdin* is the *Iliad*. By cycling through a number of repeated formulae at the beginning of individual poems, then recounting elegies for individual heroes, the whole poem sways back and forth in grief. It reminds me of the film *300*, a ritualized elegy for Spartans defeated at Thermopylae, based on Frank Miller and Lynn Varley's 1998 comic of the same name. Here is the same juxtaposition of glory and disaster, youth wielding and being cut down by violence. The colour palette – metallic glints, crimson blood and gore – is identical. Leaving its politics aside, the 1964 film *Zulu*, starring Stanley Baxter, uses the same kinds of set pieces, alternating between attention to the individual fighters' qualities and terrifying skirmishes. I find *Y Gododdin* in Welsh repetitious. That reiteration and reformulating may well be part of the drama of trying to deal with overwhelming grief but some passages are much stronger than others, making it poetically uneven.

The parallel text allows the non-Welsh-speaker to see the elaborate alliterations and repetitions of the verse. Aneirin wrote before the codification of these chimes into the strict metres of *cynghanedd*. Basil Bunting, in *Briggflatts* claimed both as his poetic fathers:

Aneurin and Taliesin, cruel owls
for whom it is never altogether dark, crying
before the rules made poetry a pedant's game.

Even in in this earlier form, the metrical complexities of the Welsh are fiendishly difficult to capture in English. This is a challenge to which Clarke is more than equal. She uses internal rhymes with virtuosity, deploys subtle off-rhymes to catch the ghost of monorhymes that go on for stanzas. She's also superb at reproducing the Welsh pattern of rhyming strong (accented) and weak (unaccented) words with each other:

When Caradog charged to war
Gored three mean like a wild boar,

Bull of the army, war machine,
He hand-fed the wolves. Owain

Son of Eulad was my witness
Before they were gone from Catraeth...

After much gold mead taken,
None saw his father again. (59)

To complement the 'Singer's Prologue, Clarke closes her Gododdin with another poem from the same manuscript but not usually counted as part of the sequence. This is 'Pais Dinogad' ('Dinogad's Coat'), a lullaby describing an absent father's exploits to his child. This adds a female voice to an entirely male poem and places both elegies and lullaby in a refreshing new context. Clarke writes: 'I hear it as one more lyric in praise of a man's courage, perhaps in the voice of a woman singing to a child in death's aftermath'.

The cumulative effect of Clarke's economical translation and her formidable poetic gifts for elegy makes this book devastating:

> Two thousand of Deifr and Brynaich's men
> Died in an hour in mire and mud and blood.
>
> Sooner meat for the wolf than to his wedding.
> Sooner carrion for the crow than priest-blessing.
> Before his burial, the field lay bleeding.
> In the hall where mead flowed free
> The poet will praise Hyfaidd Hir. (13)

The dead of Catraeth are still dead, but we have a new Aneirin to praise them.

Lyrical Thrift and Heft

Kei Miller, *Things I Have Withheld*
Canongate. £14.99
Reviewed by Douglas Field

As a poet and fiction writer, the Jamaican-born Kei Miller 'know[s] how to tell stories', but as he muses in his second collection of essays, *Things I Have Withheld*, 'but how does one begin to tell silence?' Taking his cue from the poet Dionne Brand's line that 'the most important things will be the ones I withheld', Miller pries open the vaults of silence in which things are hidden, among them sexuality, racial identity, desire, and shame. The paradox, as Miller explores across sixteen short chapters, is that 'the moment when I am most in need of words are exactly the moments when I lose faith in them and when I fall back into silence'.

Miller's essays, which are set in various geographical locations – including England, Jamaica and Scotland – underscore his resistance to fixity. The essays transgress the boundaries of the traditional essay. The volume includes two letters to the American writer James Baldwin, and one to the Kenyan writer Binyavanga Wainaina. There are autobiographical snapshots revealing long-standing family secrets; essays which are written in the style of short stories, and travel pieces about Miller's experiences in Kenya and Ethiopia. The essays, some of which are whispered, and all of which are lyrical, are threaded together by Miller's exploration of silence and the heavy weight of what is left unsaid; 'that silence in which so many things should be said are never said'. The book is populated with characters who learn that 'to share one's thoughts can be dangerous', or who strain to catch 'whispered stories', while others are 'struggling with the words'. As Miller explores the damage caused by class, racism, colourism, and homophobia, he acknowledges that 'our feelings are always so much bigger and more complex than language'.

Miller's letters to James Baldwin take on the epistolary form used by Ta-Nehisi Coates in *Between the World and Me* (2015) in which the author addresses his son, a style in turn borrowed from Baldwin's 'A Letter to My Nephew' (1962). As Miller writes to the American author whom he never met – Baldwin died in 1987 – he muses that we write letters 'as an antidote to distance, as a cure for miles and the spaces that stretch between us'. In one letter to Baldwin, Miller writes that, 'It is always the body that I return to, our bodies and their various meanings', a theme which cuts across many of the essays, among them 'The Crimes that Haunt the Body', a reflection on childhood, and 'There are Truths Hidden in Our Bodies', in which Miller acknowledges the way that 'In Britain, my black body often hides the truth of my queerness'.

Miller's economic lyricism mirrors the restraints about which he writes. In 'Absence of Poets and Poodles,' which begins in a grand Northern home – 'the kind of house that sits stoically in the present but aches towards its past' – Miller endures vexing questions from his host. 'What was it like,' he asks, 'having a talent like that and growing up in a place like Jamaica?' As Miller recalls, 'In that moment I could not say the things I wanted to say nor ask the questions I would have liked to ask, because I would have appeared rude,' and, he concludes, 'because they were too important.' In 'The Boys at the Harbour,' Miller recounts his interactions with 'The Gully Queens,' as they are nicknamed in the newspapers; homeless boys who hang out at Kingston Harbour. For the residents of New Kingston, 'these boys were squatters, prostitutes, thieves, murderers.... They were the worst of the worst.' In Miller's account, the boys emerge, not as caricatures, but as 'complicated boys in whom you could so easily lose faith.' And if you 'put your ear close to the waves of the Kingston Habour on a night when the city is sleeping ... you might hear so many stories,' Miller tells us in a passage about the 'Gully Queens.' You might hear 'stories about the cars that they have climbed into, the big men they have met – business leaders, politicians, dancehall artistes who some nights put their mouths against the mouths of these boys, kiss them so deeply, but then use the same mouths to sing terrible songs about them.'

In 'The Buck, the Bacchanal, And Again, The Body,' Miller reflects on Caribbean culture and the stories left untold. 'I sorry for the histories that haunt all of us,' Miller concludes. 'I so sorry for all them things that we find difficult to face or talk about because we wish they wasn't real... and that the things that haunt was just a figment of our over-active imaginations.' *Things I Have Withhheld* is full of ghosts; the spectres of things left unsaid – told here with quiet charisma whispered softly on the page.

Skin and Nothing

Yousif M. Qasmiyeh, *Writing the Camp* (Broken Sleep Books) £10.99
Reviewed by Shash Trevett

'Camp (n): a residue in the shape of a crescent made of skin and nothing'.

Writing the Camp is not a book you can read in one sitting. It is not even a book you can understand in one reading. It is not merely an autobiography of a poet born in Baddawi Camp in Lebanon, or a treatise on being a refugee or on the asylum system. This phenomenal collection defies easy categorisation: the poems compel the reader to question, to renegotiate, to dwell on the fluidity of memory, identity and trauma. Yousif M Qasmiyeh's language is deliberate, thought-provoking, rooted in the particular: it asks the reader to slow down, to dwell on the juxtaposition of words and ideas, to grapple with the immensities contained within the lines.

Fundamental to the collection is the question – what does it mean to 'write the camp'? Is the camp a place or an idea? Is it an extended metaphor for the act of writing itself? Is it a site for the patterning of stories? A place where the 'I' is strengthened, nourished, while simultaneously being dispersed and mutated into the other 'I's which populate the camp? In the camp time cannot exhaust itself; it is never ending, both linear and cyclical, invading and examining the lives of those living within it, opening their stories and their thresholds to the gaze of the reader. It is also the place which exists in the absence of time, where 'time died so it could return home'. Writing the camp is an attempt to record, memorialise and examine what it means to write for yourself and not be written by others. It is a site of preservation and desiccation, it is as Qasmiyeh frequently notes, an archive: 'Whoever gives birth in the camp, gives birth to the archive in the shape of flesh'.

The collection is roughly divided into three parts beginning and ending at the camp, with the middle section dealing with the refugee's journey towards citizenship in a new country. Lyrical poetry is intermixed with prose poems, the interplay between the two forms opening new avenues for thought and examination. The collection opens with a rather disquieting poem inviting the refugee arriving at the camp to 'feast upon the other to eat yourself', a theme built on later in a long sequential prose poem 'At the feast of the asylum'. A treatise on the nature of time and journeys, it presents the reader with a series of juxtaposed opposites where 'disappearances' lead to 'new undiscovered land', where the object of the journey is 'never to arrive'. The poem speaks of the negotiations refugees have to undertake, not with others, but within themselves; how in order to inhabit a present which is all too 'fluid' they have to archive a past which is solely 'governed by what [they] will say in the present'. The poem attempts to exist in both 'the time that is passing and the one that is fast approaching from all directions', while negotiating the 'time that will happen in our eyes'. The poem ends on a note of defeat: in spite of struggling to align their hemispheres, the refugee, the stranger, the one in flight 'left their time somewhere safe: where beasts gather to share their hunt'.

The multiplicity of narratives, the linguistic patterning and repetitions, the sequences of journeys and homecomings, the skillful layering of interconnectedness, of trauma and a certain religiosity of language give the collection its core strength. Figures and motifs recur: the figure of the poet's mother learning to write her name; the father building the threshold to their house; the figures of the strangers (in the Arabic understanding of the term as one who embodies the absence of the sun); the anthropologists; the cousins and family who live in neighbouring camps. The collection is preoccupied with the writing of languages and with the dialects which flow in a space which is a 'tomb that has yet to find its dead'. In a place where Kurds from Syria, Iraqis, Syrians and Palestinian live side by side, preserving the pure Palestinian dialect is a preoccupation for some. For Qasmiyeh 'the dialect is the spear of noises' that some would protect with their fists. The 'disfigured' face of the dialect is a weapon of division, of othering, where one hears only the noise of the dialect without seeing the face of the one speaking it. A sterilising force, the imposition of dialectical superiority is a marker of death: the dialect that is praised above others is never a true dialect. Instead, 'the dialect that survives on its own is that of the dead'.

Writing the Camp by its very nature is a projection of all the places that used to be, all the histories, dialects, the archives of the selves collected from a time before the camp and carried into a time which will survive the camp. To be Palestinian, writes Qasmiyeh, is to be in close proximity to the suffering of others: the scribe of an archive of suffering. Given what has happened to the people of Gaza recently, it seems all the more important to read and understand this collection; it should inform current thinking not only on the suffering of the Palestinian people, but also on all those powerless in the face of impenetrable nationalistic discourses. Qasmiyeh writes 'In my camp, women slap themselves in funerals to never let go of pain.' This book is an archive of the season of the refugee, the seasons of suffering, of dislocation, of trauma but also of the continuum of memory, of hope, of the endurance of survival. By reading it we too enter the archive of the refugee, enter the lives of people who know 'they are different in the way they measure time and water' and for a little while at least, walk in their shadow, following the tread of their cracked feet.

Entanglement

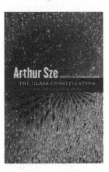

Arthur Sze, *The Glass Constellation: New and Collected Poems* (Copper Canyon Press) $35.00
Reviewed by Bonnie Costello

'Entanglement', the second of the new poems at the end of Arthur Sze's four-decade collection, begins as a mood piece. The 'you' pronoun brings the reader in close to 'listen for deer beyond / the gate', to 'toss another yellow cedar log / into the woodstove on the float house', to observe 'a great blue heron' as it 'flaps its wings, / settles on the railing.' There are many such moments of serenity in Sze's work, seemingly unremarkable scenes of pleasurable living, domesticity in tune with nature, when we 'put aside the newspaper, soak strawberry plants in a garden bed'. But such moments are almost always interrupted by remote and often dissonant images, reverberations from a wider and deeper web of existence. 'When you least expect it, your field / of vision tears, and an underlying landscape / reveals a radiating moment of time.' As particle physicists know and this poet helps us feel, the 'earth under our feet' is itself a 'float house' rocked by distant tides.

This idea of 'entanglement', though it goes by different names, underlies much of Sze's poetry, and gives it at once ontological, moral, and scientific dimensions. The poet who began his education at MIT understands that the world is not a collection of discrete, solid objects, but a trembling web, a structure of relations of surprising, non-contingent correlations and impacts. Sze's particular locality has been for many years Santa Fe, New Mexico, where he was Director of the Museum of Native American Arts, and where he still makes his home. As a learned naturalist, gardener and avid hiker, he knows this terrain. He has affinities to Gary Snyder and A.R Ammons, to Forrest Gander. But no other contemporary poet has done as much to bring readers into the precise landscape and daily life of the Southwest – its arroyos and acequias, its petroglyphs on sandstone, its cacti, rattle snakes and lizards, its night skies; but also its strip malls, its gas stations and pick-up trucks, its strung out or pent up population, its Native and Hispanic heritage. His 'here' also, though, includes places from memory and imagination – travels up and down the American west coast, to China, India, Greece – as they penetrate our immediate sense awareness, creating at once an immediate and manifold of sense of being.

The son of Chinese immigrants, Sze is a distinguished translator of Chinese poetry, and Asian poetic and philosophical traditions. Image-based juxtaposition, openness to chance, ego-shattering and interrogative thought, remain central to this practice. The empirical and theoretical knowledge of the physical world, of which Sze has a remarkable range, enriches rather than competes with our emotional engagement. Theorems of geometry and physics (as in 'The Angle of Reflection Equals the Angle of Incidence') are pondered as much for their spiritual as for their epistemological potential. This is a fresh kind of environmental imagination, with none of the stagy Thoreauvian 'contact' with unmediated Nature, or Emersonian summation of the 'All'. And yet, with full humility and wonder, the sense of the sublime does often arise, with its perplexing interplay of the minute and the vast, and its mixture of pleasure and terror, order and rupture. Sometimes it arises in a local image that finds radiance in the everyday: 'men unload / sardines in a burst of argentine light'; sometimes in a conceptual paradox arising from baffled awareness: 'though parallel lines touch in the infinite, the infinite is here – '

Like many poets, Sze found his proper form gradually. Perhaps this is why,– though he has been publishing poetry since the early seventies – he begins his *Collected Poems* mid-career, with a selection from exhilarating *Redshifting Web*, a 1998 volume, backing up to the chronology forty pages in. Sze's earliest poetry tends toward simple declarative statements in present tense, and elemental imagery of moon, bird, sea, fish, and plums. His mature style relies less on a central guiding persona; shifting pronouns create a prismatic orientation that sees there are 'so many / worlds to this world'. 'Redshift' is a term from astronomy, denoting the lengthening waves of light that define objects in space in relation to perceivers. In these poems there are many angles of vision within that collective 'us' though Sze maintains an inclusive poise and balance in the meditations.

Parataxis has been the dominant rhetorical mode in modern American poetry for a century, and it can sometimes feel lax. In the radical parataxis and juxtaposition of Sze's mature style, 'bits of consciousness constellate', even when, as in some poems, we have only a list. Beyond astronomy, he explores a range of other organizing metaphors for gathered but open-ended multiplicity – archipelagos, apache plumes, quipu knots, crystal strings, among others. Certain objects and shapes repeat to form patterns and associations – hummingbirds are ubiquitous, for instance, and zigzag lines recur; water and gold light wash through many scenes. Like most cataloguing poets, Sze is fond of anaphora: one Whitmanian sentence carries us through present participles, 'dropping', 'pulling', 'filling', 'flaring', 'slicing', 'germinating'. Another binds the local to the cosmic as the word 'Here' darts over the page from 'skid marks on I 25' to 'the origin of starlight'. In 'Quipu', Sze adopts the ancient Mayan form of calculation, a nonlinear system using knots on a rope as memes: 'the mind ties knots, and I / follow a series of short strings to a loose end'. The rhetorical strategies for repetition vary from one section to the next in the 'quipu' sequencing; in one it is a series of questions, each occupying a line; in another it is a series of 'as' clauses. Such structures organize but do not box in perception. The poet lays down cairns on a path that is infinite.

Like movements in music, Sze's poems are often in

finely woven sequences – sometimes occupying a dozen pages in the later volumes. These are held together through recurrences and refrains. This practice becomes prominent with *Compass Rose* where Sze introduces 'hinge' poems – two-line intervals of apparently unrelated images that become subtly iconic and are picked up and repeated pages later. The technique is most striking in the title poem of 'Sight Lines', which works as a kind of self-referential cento, built almost entirely out of lines in previous poems in the book.

While there are sonorous lines throughout, and a sense of rhythm and pacing, Sze's organic design of stanzas and white space is a matter of the eye more than the ear. Lines of equal length, in ones or twos, or alternates of ones and twos, sometimes in fours or fives, some justified prose poem blocks, others in three-line stairways, create frames for a heterogeneous vision. Enjambment is rare and therefore meaningful when it arises, creating drama and suspension ('a droplet of water hangs at the tip of a fern – water / spills into another kettle') or opening up phrasal alternatives: 'the moon slides from partial to full / to partial and then into emptiness; but no // moon's in the sky, just slanting sunlight'.

Sze's rich and diverse lexicon delights and challenges, but is never merely ornamental and, at the same time, creates aural texture: 'agapanthuses are opening umbels / of violet flowers' and an 'oologist' distinguishes 'finch eggs from wren or sparrow'; the poet glimpses 'a trogon between ovate leaves' or advises the reader to 'feel [...] the ocarina of your body'. Sze does more than collect nouns. He often converts them into verbs, showing how we might find ourselves in nature, our possibilities and our defenses, rather than merely projecting ourselves onto it: 'ensuing loss salamanders the body, lagoons the mind'.

In the most recent volumes lines are sometimes cancelled, exposing the poet's imperfect process, his ambivalence, but also his struggle against negativity from within as well as without. In the voice of a Chinese water-calligrapher he lets 'the brush ~~swerve~~ rest' and makes:

> the one ~~stroke~~ hook – ah, it's all
> in that hook – there, I levitate: no mistakes
> will last, even regret is lovely – my hand
> trembles; but I find the ~~gaps~~ resting places.[. . .
> . . .] I smile, ~~frown~~
> fidget, let go – I draw the white, not the black –

Human nature is caught in errancy, in rhythms of destruction and creation that are not strictly redemptive. In *Sight Lines* Arthur Sze achieved a new level of eloquence, a musical and aphoristic resonance that makes his late work his most memorable. And the new poems of 'The White Orchard' at the end of *The Glass Constellation* show that he is writing from strength to strength, steering us, without dogma, toward a better, gentler course in our relations with each other and the earth.

A Message from my Wife

Charles Boyle, *The Disguise, Poems 1977–2001*, selected by Christopher Reid (Carcanet) £12.99; *The Late Sun*, Christopher Reid (Faber) £14.99
Reviewed by Edmund Prestwich

The Disguise is a selection from the six volumes Charles Boyle published between 1977 and 2001, when he apparently stopped writing poetry. As he puts it in the Author's Note, 'I was writing poems I had *already written*, so I got off the bike.'

You can't argue with a decision like that but you can regret it. The poems Christopher Reid has selected are remarkably good.

'Moving In', the first poem from Boyle's first book, opens arrestingly, 'The shape of the key is still strange in my hand.' Its abrupt, luminous particularity is typical of Boyle's style. So is the sense of the speaker's alienation from what he sees and even from the person he addresses. He speaks to someone who seems to be a partner but she seems almost as strange to him as the house they're moving into, that they 'wander through, touching dust, pausing / to look, to listen, to watch each other's faces.' Poems from the first three books are indeed largely set abroad but the sense of estrangement seems to reflect something fundamental to the poet's way of seeing the world. The fourth poem, 'Alex in February', ends 'Exile's a disease. We catch it being born'. One way in which Boyle develops is that estrangement becomes more radical and more obviously a stylistic choice.

A delightful early poem like 'Shy Mountain Children' gets its life from the sensation that although there's an unbridgeable gap between the speaker and his companion, on the one hand, and the children on the other, there's eagerness for contact too. The hard-edged brilliance of the later poems depends on the way they make contact seem simply impossible. The other characters in these poems are often people known through books, like D.H. Lawrence or characters from Stendhal, so that everything in the poem happens at a double remove from reality. In several, different levels of reality or unreality swirl round each other, as in 'Timur the Lame', in which a lame beggar becomes the medieval Mongol war-leader speaking of cairns of skulls and the wind off the steppes. In 'Eadweard Muybridge' the apparently true circumstances of Muybridge's murder of his wife's lover are weird enough to achieve the effect of unreality simply by being related in a flat, deadpan way and mixed with other facts from Muybridge's career.

What makes these anecdotes initially gripping is the jolt of strangeness itself. What gives them lasting effect is sheer technical skill – sharp observation, concentrated language, the sense of being immediately addressed by an individual speaker, the concision with which he presents the essentials of a situation and the momentum with which he develops it:

'My name is Muybridge,' said the night-time visitor,
'and I have a message for you from my wife.'
Then he fired a single shot …

In the later collections Boyle refuses even implicit interpretation of his arresting anecdotes. This leaves them lingering in the mind and teasing the imagination.

Reid's stance in relation to his readers is opposite to Boyle's. He bubbles away disarmingly with an air of relaxed but well-mannered familiarity. Where Boyle suppresses comment, Reid's poems are suffused both with what offer themselves as frank statements of opinion and with transparently opinionative language.

Some of the poems are formally elaborate, and Reid shows considerable technical skill in constructing them according to demanding specifications while maintaining an airily conversational tone. In such poems I found myself delighting in the eloquence of his phrasing, the way he kept ideas dancing through difficult hoops, creating wider and wider ripples of association in the process. Sometimes I wondered whether they were more than beautifully spun trifles, like the bubbles you see street performers making with tri-string wands, delightful to read but inherently ephemeral because the focus going through them was so much on pleasure in Reid's fast-moving, apparently effortless rising to the challenges he'd set himself. Reading a poem by Boyle, in contrast, left a residue of strong images and a vivid narrative arc.

In other poems, especially unrhymed ones, serious reflections are subtly moulded in with the lightness and wit of the overt sense. Three clear examples of poems with such hinted depths are 'Boomers', which mixes comedy with pity and ruefulness as it surveys gracelessly aging 'enormous male babies'; 'Running at the Sea', in which tender description of two children playing with the sea hints, in an unobtrusive way, at the ambiguity of our relations with the nonhuman nature we emerge from and will ultimately be overwhelmed by; and 'The Frost-Fox', which describes a dead vixen on Reid's dead mother's lawn. When he's buried her, all that's left is 'the grass-green silhouette of a vixen / nimbly stepping forth / to meet her fortune'. The application to the mother is poignant but unstated, a shadow sense accompanying the explicit thrust of the poem. And the emphasis on sheer joy in the more purely playful pieces gets its apologia in the final poem, 'The Late Sun' itself, in which Reid says of the spreading of light one dawn, 'To watch was to take / a lesson in light and being alive.' Altogether, for the lover of formal verse, this book gives considerable pleasure though some people – emphatically not including me – may find its world too middle class and culturally elitist for them to relate to.

Blessed and Cursed

Iain Crichton Smith, *Deer on the High Hills: Selected Poems*, edited by John Greening (Carcanet £14.99)
Reviewed by Andrew McNeillie

Iain Crichton Smith was one of the remarkable Scottish poets of his time and it was a time rich in poets of distinction. (He is figured in Sandy Moffat's iconic group portrait *Poets' Pub* along with the other Makars of the age that Hugh MacDiarmid brought together.) Smith is only one among them, by the way, who owe the heart of their posterity to Carcanet.

Poets generally cannot choose the language they write in. The Muse makes them monoglots. R.S. Thomas, with whose poetry Smith's has something in common (listen for a particular example to 'Poem of Lewis' which opens this selection), could write prose in Welsh but not a poetry. The Muse blessed Smith with two tongues, Gaelic and English. I am not qualified to say that he was in his poetry (he wrote fiction in Gaelic and English too) equally adept in both languages, but others better placed, including Sorley MacLean, have made it clear that he was. That in itself is startling.

Otherwise in much of his early life and circumstances, Smith was singularly unblessed. Indeed, he was cursed, by breadline poverty and the oppressive character of his mother, widowed when the poet was one year old. She, for her sins, adhered to the deadly Wee Free version of Protestantism. Throughout her life, the poet was extraordinarily caring of this grim soul, at great cost to his sanity, which in the end broke down, for a desperate time, after her death. 'Blessed and Cursed' could almost be the title of one of his books. He loved to hold opposites up to each other. Yet in person he was truly a blessing and inspiration to meet, as many have testified. So he is to read.

Born in Glasgow, Smith was still in his cradle when his mother removed to her (and her late husband's) native Lewis. She settled in the village of Bayble, a name, as is commonly observed, at once suggestive to ear and eye of Babel and Bible. What a place to be taken to. What a place to come from. Smith came from it to an education at Aberdeen and then to work as a schoolmaster, eventually in Oban. The schoolroom afforded him setting and context for some fine poems. But if he was any one thing, he was a poet of place, and of what, writing on Derek Walcott, Joseph Brodsky called the 'outskirts' of Empire. Though Lewis is the farthest cry from a Caribbean paradise. Empire, and the consequences of Empire, loomed over its wilderness from a glowering sky, and strode through it stamping out, or scattering, its language as it went.

Emigration, the Clearances and the plight of the Gaelic language, provide vital subjects and contexts for many of Smith's poems. (See 'Culloden and After', 'The Clearances', 'Shall Gaelic Die?' and see the quirky but intriguing 'For Poets Writing in English over in Ireland' in which both Philip Larkin and Douglas Dunn have walk-on parts.) John Greening represents these well with astute selections. But insofar as Smith is a poet of place and 'landscape', he is a poet of the folk and everyday realism (sometimes with a dash of a yellow surrealism) rather than Nature. (See for example 'Return to the Council House'.) He relished with some panache the alienation effects that forays into popular culture can produce. We overlook his range of subject (Greening gets it right) at our peril. His novelist's, his story-teller's insight into character and psychology, his gift for storytelling, all nourish and enrich his poems. He is a subtle, often wryly, sometimes dourly humorous, observer of the human. As Greening urges us to acknowledge, Smith could also tackle big international political issues with lasting success (see the 'Against Apartheid II' selected here).

Smith's take on the natural world is directly grounded in the materialist Celtic tradition not the Romantic. Perhaps nothing in his work expresses this better than the poem 'Deer on the High Hills', perfectly chosen for this selection's title. Behind the poem (and within in it) stands the great work 'Praise of Ben Dorain' by the illiterate Gaelic bard Duncan Bàn MacIntyre (1724–1812). Smith produced a distinguished translation of this lengthy 'pibroch' poem (see his *Collected Poems*). It cannot be sensibly excerpted, though Greening proves himself most adept at giving effective 'chunks' from other longer poems.

Smith's deer are, as deer may seem: flighty, skittish, inhuman, dangerous, 'balanced on delicate logic'. His opening couplet – 'A deer looks through you to the other side / and what it sees is an inhuman pride' – holds in little the delicate and paradoxical logic of the whole poem to come, a XIV-part work of loosely rhymed Dantean stanzas. The deer are inhuman. What can be their pride? As Gertrude Stein would have said, a deer is a deer is a deer is a deer. But that won't do, and being human we want more. So enter the winter ballroom from the mountain heights, our old friend anthropomorphism to dance a reel with the wild. I say dance but it's more a stand-off. And what a 'wild' it becomes, full of delightful simile and inspired allusion. Smith's deer on frozen ground are like 'debutantes on a smooth ballroom floor'. Like Louis XVI, they have 'the inhuman look of aristocrats / before a revolution comes'; they are on history's thin ice; they take to the hills 'with great bounding leaps like the mind of God'. There is no idea it seems they cannot leap us to. Here are Hector and Ulysses and that hint of Homeric realism that knows the nature of Nature on those stark terms we have forgotten, but Bàn MacIntyre (also present) had not, nor Smith, quite, who would hold our human nature up against them. Edwin Morgan thought the poem one of Smith's poorer productions. For him it made too much of too little and had too much Wallace Stevens in its nostrils. It's ironic but his criticisms somewhat echo those Smith made concerning MacDiarmid's stones in his great poem 'On a Raised Beach'. Here is an interesting way-in to this fine volume.

There are many possible points of entry to this prolific poet. John Greening has given us the best anyone could wish for.

The Space Between

Kirsty Gunn and Gail Low, *Imagined Spaces* (The Voyage Out Press) £14.99
Reviewed by Iain Bamforth

It's curious how collections of essays nearly always devote space, in the introduction or among the contents, to defining exactly what the essay is – as if it suffered from a crisis of legitimacy despite having been a literary form for four hundred years, or more troublingly, as if editors are unsure readers will recognise an essay when presented with one. Perhaps the currently hobbled forms of public discourse on what is euphemistically known as the social media have a role to play in this phenomenon. Like the novel, the essay has been proclaimed dead; yet both forms thrive, and have even been known to cross-fertilise: the 'personal essay' promises to tell the whole truth and nothing but the truth whereas nothing, but nothing, is guaranteed true in the 'fictional essay'.

Imagined Spaces, a publication from Dundee's Voyage Out Press and edited by Kirsty Gunn and Gail Low, is no exception to this rule, and also provides examples of these new hybrid and crossover forms. Dundee, Scotland's fourth and possibly most overlooked city, home to literary talents as diverse as W.N. Herbert and Don Paterson, is a significant presence in the book. It opens with its editors walking across the Tay bridge, observing 'the river's flat-calm grey, rendered in a dull sheen by the low light' and developing an analogy between the span of the bridge and the span of words that 'glint and teem'. Dundee's striking setting on the edge of the Tay was not lost on the trustees of the V&A who were persuaded that construction of the first design museum in Scotland would spur regeneration of the city's waterfront. Susan Nickalls's essay 'Mind the Gap' provides a fascinating account of the life and aesthetics of the Japanese architect Kengo Kuma, who won the competition to build what is now an unmissable urban landmark, a building that is 'hard on the outside, soft on the inside'.

In discussing Kuma's aesthetics Nickalls opens up the Japanese concept of 'ma', the gap between notes in music or particles in space. This seems, unwittingly, to have been recruited as a structural element in Stephen Carruthers and Fiona Stirling's exchange 'You by Me: Writing Depression' which attempts, in a kind of agonistic personal essay, to batter a way through the thicket of definitions applied to mental health problems. Writing depression, not writing *about* depression: once named, a feeling is no longer the same feeling. It becomes a concept and calls forth further definition, in what Ian Hacking termed the 'looping effect': the authors' use of typographic effect to express nuances suggests that this kind of reflexiveness may not have any exits at all. 'What if we're in a circle, you and I?' This kind of unboundedness/prisoner's dilemma seems expressive of our present 'always connected' reality. Meaghan Delahunt in her thoughtful 'Life in the Bardo: Dying, Death and the Imagination' is concerned with how creating coincides with letting go: her token figure is the Japanese artist Motoi Yamamoto, who makes 'saltworks' – intricate installations at the end of which he invites members of the public to collect the salt in containers and return it to the sea as a ritual gesture.

Intransitivity is a feature of Linda Chown's piece 'The Art of the Intransitive Essay', which widens what she calls 'bethinking': her discovery that she only began to appreciate Montaigne when she realised how much she struggled 'with *how* to think far more than with *what* to think.' Her sense of bonding, 'across centuries and persons', carries over in many other contributions to this collection: the exchange on 'exploring the fiction of writing in the academy in the twenty-first century' by Emma Bolland and Elizabeth Chakrabarty, the exchange of letters between Duncan McLean and Kenny Taylor about 'northness' and the half-forgotten Danish author Sigrid Undset, the conversation between Lorens Holm and Paul Noble (accompanied by photographs) about the social and civic ideas of Patrick Geddes (another Dundee luminary and an environmentalist long before the word became fashionable), and in the exploration of home and away, alternative languages (Urdu, Yoruba, Scots, English) and identities, by Tomiwa Folorunso and Hamzah Hussain. Where? becomes as important as Who?

A formally more conventional but gripping essay is provided by Dai John, who talks about his work in the British military during the 'ops' in Kosovo and the Helmand Valley and queries his lifelong 'journal-keeping habit'. His idea of 'getting home' is quite different from that of Folorunso and Hussain, because it spells the end of the intimacy of hardship and dangers faced in the field. His imaginings of the familiar have made it strange to him. Two distinguished writers also make appearances. Gabriel Josipovici discourses briefly on 'being hit on the head by a poem' (specifically the 'liquid siftings' of T.S. Eliot's 'Sweeney among the Nightingales') and the American essayist Phillip Lopate, whose anthology *The Art of the Personal Essay* made him a 'promotional' figure for the genre, reflects on how 'the essay has long been neglected on a theoretical level' in spite of undergoing 'something of a revival'. (Twenty years ago, he notes, publishers tried to avoid mention of the signifier 'essays' on their book covers.)

This brings us back to the starting point: defining the essay. Lopate argues that while the essay's 'often-cited elements include its extraordinary flexibility and mutability, its literary sparkle, its undogmatic, anti-methodical, anti-totalising tendencies, its tropism towards ambivalence, doubt, skepticism, self-mockery, its free-

dom to wander and digress, its cockroach-like resilience and survival ability', all these characterisations are idealising and self-approving. He cautions that the essay – etymologically an experiment, an assay, a line taken for a walk (Paul Klee) – should not allow its liberty to become laxity: woolly-headedness or moral preachiness are all around us. Klee's exhortation has also encouraged the editors of this appealing book to include a series of ink wash studies by the multimedia artist Whitney McVeigh, which, halfway between Chinese rice-paper calligraphy and Henri Michaux's zoomorphic 'apparitions', suggest how the essayistic can also find palimpsestic expression in the visual domain.

Through a Temperament

Ian McMillan, *Yes But What Is This? What Exactly?* (Smith Doorstop) £4.50
Richie McCaffery, *First Hare* (Mariscat Press) £6.00
Anna Selby, *Field Notes* (Hazel Press) £10.00
Daniel Fraser, *Iron Lung* (Ignition Press) £5.00
Reviewed by Rory Waterman

According to Émile Zola, and in what I think equals any other necessarily watery definition, art is 'life seen through a temperament'. As anyone reading this will know, Ian McMillan's public temperament – usually on full display in his poetry – is warm, wry, mischievous. His style hasn't developed much over the decades, though the same might be said of A. E. Housman, Wendy Cope, Philip Larkin, Tony Harrison, and any number of other poets with huge readerships. Rather, each of his collections contains more or fewer poems one wants to mark and remember. *Yes But What Is This? What Exactly?* – the answer to which might be 'what you'd expect it to be' – has an unusually high hit rate.

All the world is a stage for McMillan, and most performances contain elements of farce. In 'Seeing a Goal Scored from a Passing Train', 'A bloke who looks like he is made of mud / Boots the ball', 'The keeper flaps like a scarf in the breeze', and 'I stand and whoop and the train's dullards / Stare at me like I'm a cave painting come to life'. In 'The News', a dog on 'one of / Those long leads that stretch / To Doncaster' says 'Who's voting Tory on Thursday? / I know I am!' He can be poignant, though – as in 'Ten Der', a beautiful little poem built around repetitions and focused on a woman cutting flowers to 'The sound of tender / Murmurings / That could be song'; or 'Three Flat Caps at the Bottom of the Stairs', about the mining industry ('what a bastard'): 'Notice this: saying years and years piles them up, / Piles years on years like the coal the wagons // Used to pile outside the house'.

Richie McCaffery is also apparently quite self-absorbed, though he is a very different sort of poet. I tend to think of him (somewhat reductively) as a modern, Northumbrian Wordsworth: full of bucolic non-whimsy and human insight, with not a joke in sight:

You asked me why, in the village
and fields where I grew up,
there are large blue barrels –
They're pheasant feeders, I said.

You told me: *That's so kind!*
[...]
Our love fattens itself daily
unaware of greater schemes at play.

These poems are so plainspoken that the frequent moments of feeling and tension stick out with the salience of mountains from a plain. When it doesn't come off, the effect is inevitably underwhelming; but frequently it does, and after two collections and two pamphlets McCaffery is increasingly assured, in an unobtrusive voice all his own. There are lots of childhood memories of 'vague village life' in *First Hare*: a mother at Sports Day, between her three jobs, 'cheering me on as I came last'; a grandfather who fought in North Africa during the War and wouldn't talk about it, but who would sing 'a cradle song in Arabic' or 'let me use his medals / to make stars in my Plasticine'. Such anecdotal verse would be killed by overwriting, and McCaffery has developed a knack for leaving it up to us to find the parallels in his tempered, pithy, frequently memorable poems.

Anna Selby's *Field Notes* really are, essentially, field notes. As she notes in a note on the notes: 'the finished poems all began outdoors with field notes of flora, fauna and water, done from 40ft below to 12,198ft above sea-level.' These are contrasted with the more purely notelike, less fieldy 'Notes from the Water', comprising the pamphlet's middle third: 'jottings, thoughts, observations of different marine environments and species written on waterproof notebooks with pencil, in and under the Atlantic [...]. They are presented in the order they were made and transcribed as they were written.' We'll have to take her word for that, though admittedly they don't feel particularly honed: 'Sardines. Hundreds of them at one point. I swim in the centre of them – Cornelia Parker's shed at the Tate modern, blown apart. All their whitenesses together. Suspended. A tree full with leaves. Invisible branches. Paisley.' Much as it is intriguing to read the quantum-leaping thoughts of an agile submerged mind, we're often left wondering which right image a poem might have settled on. The other two thirds of the pamphlet is simply richer: concentrated, as well as pellucid and frequently disorienting. Consider 'Arrowhead Hammock', in which 'My first run since the abortion' is the frame through which everything in the poem must be seen:

                        an American
herring gull flies along the tide-line

a crab in its beak
Ganesh-like, upturned limbs

curling to cloud and sun, a complicated figure
in the straightforward, slow shape of a seabird

the cargo drops on the rocks
a dog exalts in the carcasses

Or 'Sea Cucumbers', about both perceived and real threats that might hide under both literal and metaphorical surfaces: 'I study leopard-spotted sea cucumbers / fat, thick, huge as porno cocks in the greasy water': here we are '40ft below' sea-level as promised, presumably. When she re-emerges, 'The harbour men / flick their cigarettes, staring / starting down the steps.'

I'll end with a beginning: Daniel Fraser's debut, *Lung Iron*, chockfull of awkward insights into urban life and its dislocations. Fraser is an exceptionally limpid and assured writer – considerably more assured than the persona in most of the poems, grappling with life's slippery, knotted rope. Sometimes his irony is a little heavily wrought – 'The rumble of Truth's winged oaks, torn mad // by the braying dogs of modernity' is a dully elevated way to describe the apparent 'disenchantment' of London's Gospel Oak to Barking Overground line – but he undermines it well, which is a habit. Later in the same poem: '*Don't get mythic*, the man in the lemon polo / implies, reading his tattoo out loud.' Like McMillan – at least here, and thus far – Fraser is a wry observer of others, though his is a more metropolitan, allusive, and multi-registered voice: the older poet would never choose to write something like 'I stole that line from Samuel Beckett, / Who half-inched it himself from Saint Gerome, / Fenced on the way by Boswell's Life of Johnson', though Fraser does self-consciously end that quatrain with the McGonagallian 'A brutal crime committed by such an extraordinary tome.' What startles most about Fraser, though, is his frequent eye for detail, and his deftness at applying that to human predicaments large and small, real and surreal: 'the coffin lending you a weight / you never could have carried', or:

flushed pink and drunk on bubbles we squatted
in the outdoor pool, ankle-deep and under-lit,

crowded with *froufrou* ferns, the atmosphere
seedy and oxygenated: a plump swamp.

A couple in matching swimwear sidled crabwise
along the shallow pit, eyes secreting

indecent proposals, a whiff of gin
and car keys. We scuttled out in seconds,

back to safe sex and unbranded cava [...].

Some Contributors

Vona Groarke's eighth poetry collection, *Link*, will be published in October by Gallery Books. **Theodore Ell** is an Australian writer and editor whose poetry, essays and translations have been published in Australia, Italy and Lebanon. His biography of Italian poet Piero Bigongiari, *A Voice in the Fire,* was published in 2015. He is an Honorary Lecturer in literature at the Australian National University. **Alice Hiller**'s debut, *bird of winter*, explores living beyond being groomed and sexually abused in childhood. Her PhD is from UCL. She curates the estate of the sculptor Oscar Nemon. **Sean O'Brien**'s tenth collection, *It Says Here*, was published by Picador in 2020. He has edited Alistair Elliot's *This is the Life: Selected Poems,* which is to appear later this year from Shoestring Press. He is Professor of Creative Writing at Newcastle University. **Jonathan Simons** is the founding editor of offline publishing house Analog Sea and its literary journal, *The Analog Sea Review*. To receive a free copy of The Analog Sea Bulletin, send a letter or postcard to Analog Sea at Basler Strasse 115, 79115 Freiburg, Germany. **Alex Wong** has published two collections of verse, *Poems Without Irony* (2016) and *Shadow and Refrain* (2021). He teaches English at Cambridge, where his Russian-speaking collaborators, **Anna Ivaskevica** and **Alex Chernova**, have both at different times studied with him. **Patrick McGuinness**'s latest book is *Real Oxford* (Seren), an exploration of the city beyond the dreaming spires. **David Herman** is a freelance writer based in London and has been a regular contributor to *PN Review* since 2011. **James Womack** lives unwillingly in Cambridge. His most recent collection, *Homunculus*, was published in 2020. **John Fuller**'s latest collection of poems is *Awake & Asleep* (Chatto and Windus, 2020). Shoestring Press published his short thriller *Loser* earlier this year. **Andrew McNeillie** edits the journal *Archipelago*, devoted to 'the unnameable archipelago'of Britain and Ireland. His *Striking a Match in a Storm: Collected Poems* is due from Carcanet in March 2022. **Robyn Marsack** is Chair of StAnza's Board of Trustees, and is working on family history relating to World War I. **Jeffrey Wainwright**'s most recent book is *As Best We Can* (Carcanet 2020). A *New and Collected Poems* is in preparation. He is also the author of *Poetry the Basics* (Routledge, third edition) and *Responsible Speech: Essays on the Poetry of Geoffrey Hill* (MUP). **Joshua Weiner**'s translation of Nelly Sachs' *Flight and Metamorphosis* will be published by Farrar Straus Giroux in 2022. He lives in Washington D.C. **Douglas Field** is Senior Lecturer in Twentieth Century American Literature at the University of Manchester. He is the author of several books on James Baldwin. **Jena Schmitt**'s essays, poetry, short fiction and drawings have appeared in journals in the UK, Canada and the US. **Bonnie Costello** is Warren Distinguished Professor at Boston University and the author of books and articles on modern poetry, most recently *The Plural of Us: Poetry and Community in Auden and Others*. She also publishes creative nonfiction.

Colophon

Editors
Michael Schmidt
John McAuliffe

Editorial Manager
Andrew Latimer

Contributing Editors
Vahni Capildeo
Sasha Dugdale
Will Harris

Design
by Andrew Latimer

Editorial address
The Editors at the address on the right. Manuscripts cannot be returned unless accompanied by a stamped addressed envelope or international reply coupon.

Trade distributors
NBN International

Represented by
Compass IPS Ltd

Copyright
© 2021 Poetry Nation Review
All rights reserved
ISBN 978-1-80017-068-1
ISBN 0144-7076

Subscriptions—6 issues
 INDIVIDUAL–print and digital:
£39.50; abroad £49
 INSTITUTIONS–print only:
£76; abroad £90
 INSTITUTIONS–digital only:
from Exact Editions (https://shop.exacteditions.com/gb/pn-review)
to: PN Review, Alliance House, 30 Cross Street, Manchester, M2 7AQ, UK.

Supported by